Kindness Is Cool
(No More Bullying)

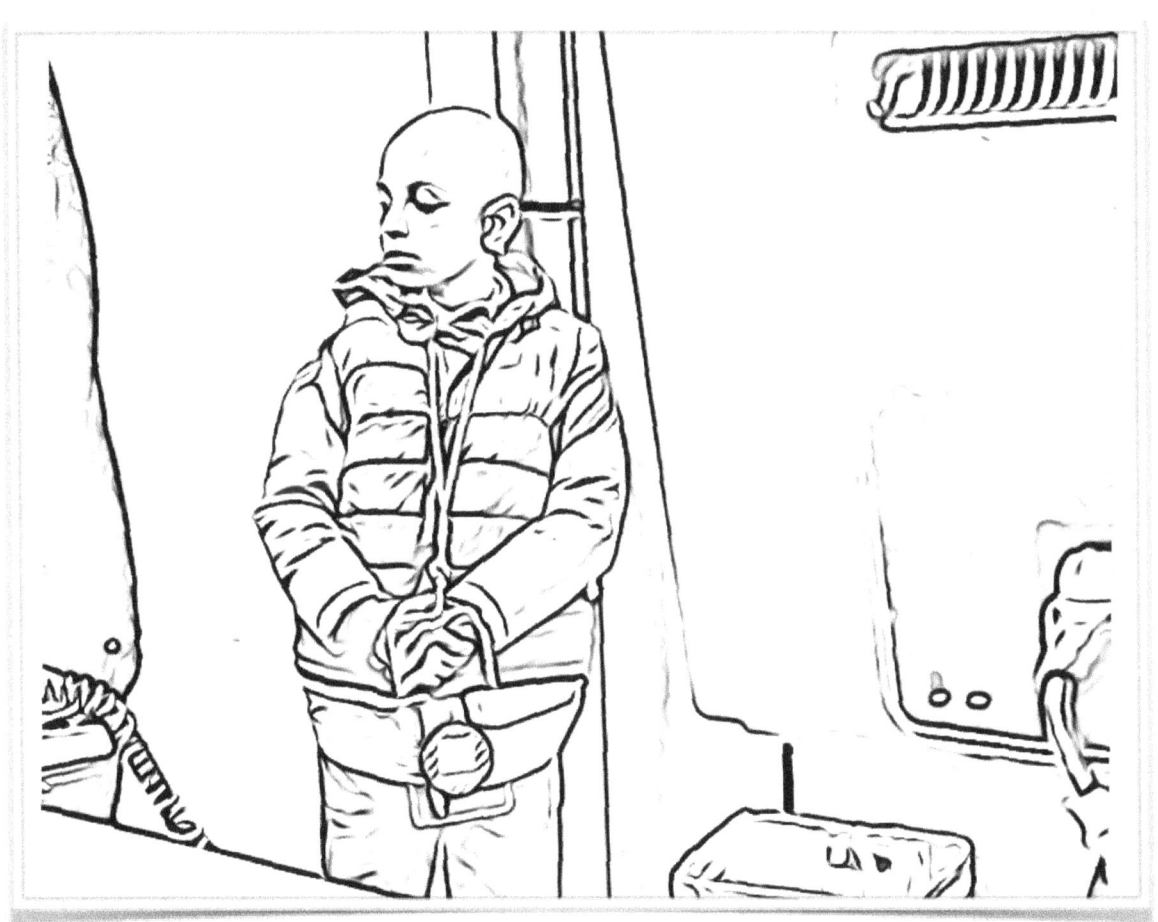

Coloring with Kindness

Kindness Is An Approach To Bullying not a Reaction

Kindness is considering in advance how other people feel and using your words, influence and actions to build them up positively. Bullying is the exact opposite, using your words, actions and influence negatively to devalue people. You don't wake up one day and decide I want to be a bully. Things happen that impact us emotionally and mentally. With the high rate of suicides in our nation it's time to color in the blurred lines of bullying with Kindness. Let's make Kindness Cool **again**.

Kindness Is Cool (No More Bullying)

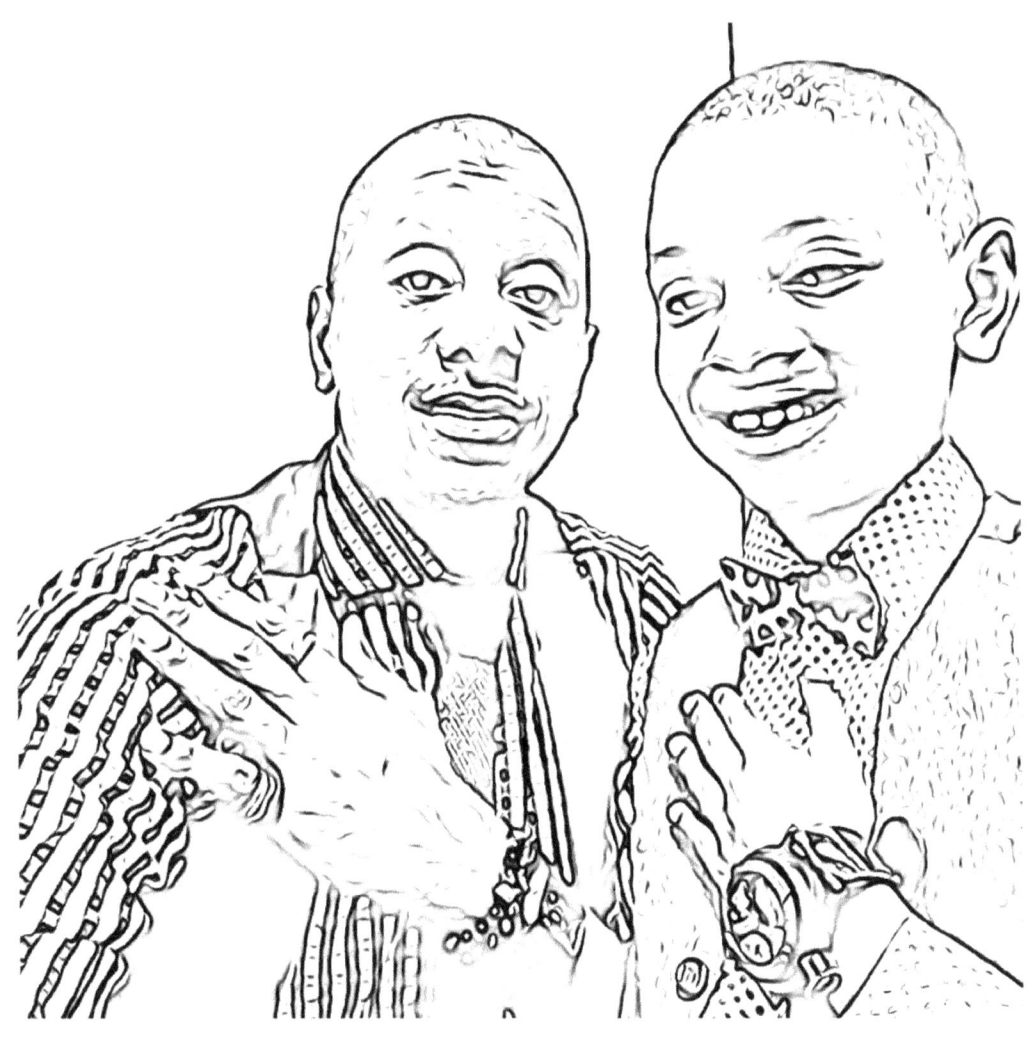

Your attitude is not an accident, but the family you're raised in allows you to be this happy person.

1. What do you love about your family?

2. What would you change about your family?

3. What makes you happy?

4. What does it mean to have a good attitude?

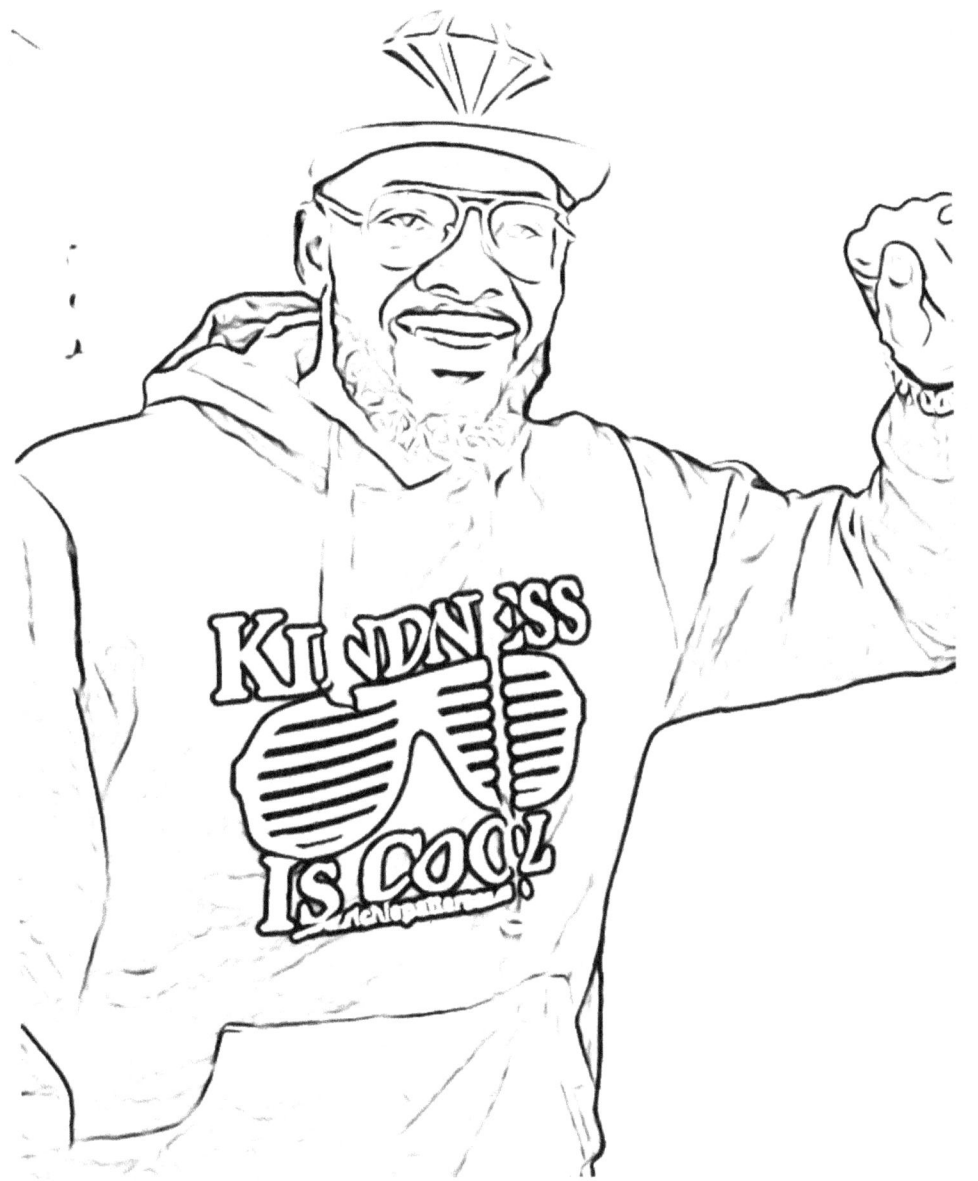

Some will say having a one parent home doesn't matter, but we need all hands on deck to stop bullying. Dad has to be able to teach Kindness in a way that offenses can be resolved.

1. What's the hardest thing for your mom or dad to understand about bullying?

2. What would you say to mom or dad about bullying if you could tell them anything?

3. What does Kindness mean to you?

4. When was the last time you expressed Kindness towards someone in the last 90 days?

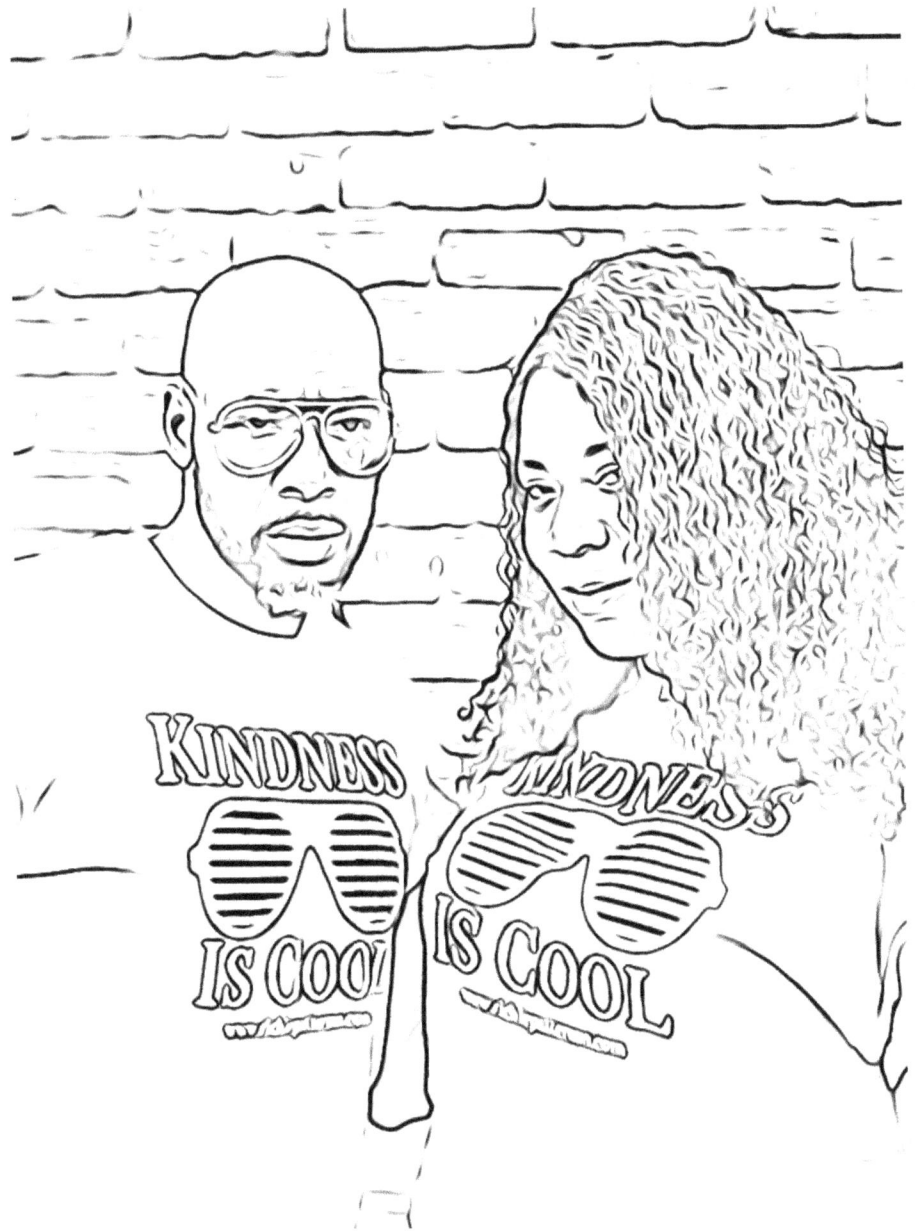

Some of us come from two parent homes and that's a good thing. The beauty of a two parent home is that there can be more validation and open ended conversations to increase your confidence.

1. Who shows you what Kindness looks like where you live?

2. What does acceptance mean to you?

3. What is confidence?

4. What words do you love to hear most from Mom or Dad?

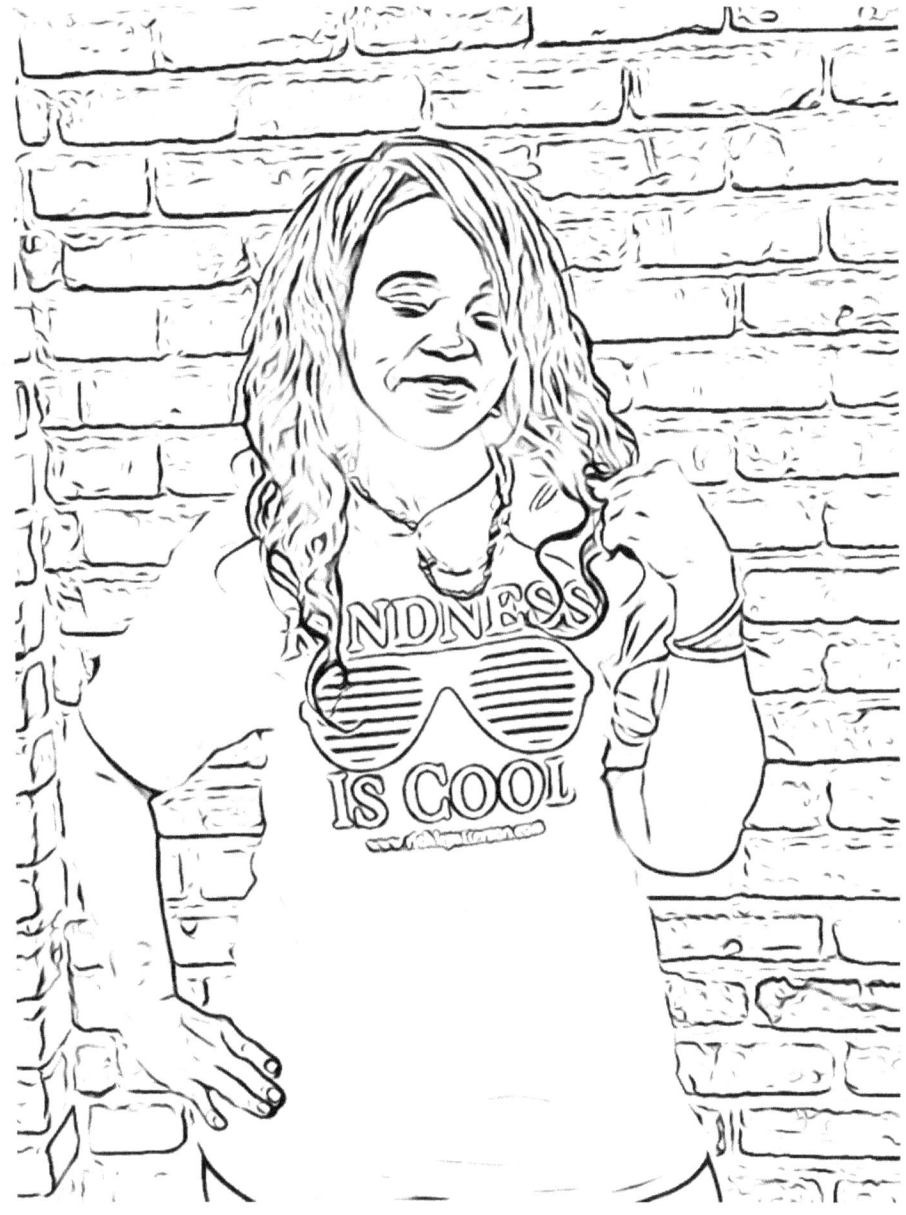

Mom is at every parent teacher conference and is engaged at home, but she can't be everywhere at the same time. Even the greatest mom needs some help with understanding bullying.

1. What does mom need to know about bullying that she may not know?

2. Name three things that mom or your guardian say that make you feel better?

3. What is the best memory you have together with your mom or guardian?

Kindness Is Cool (No More Bullying)

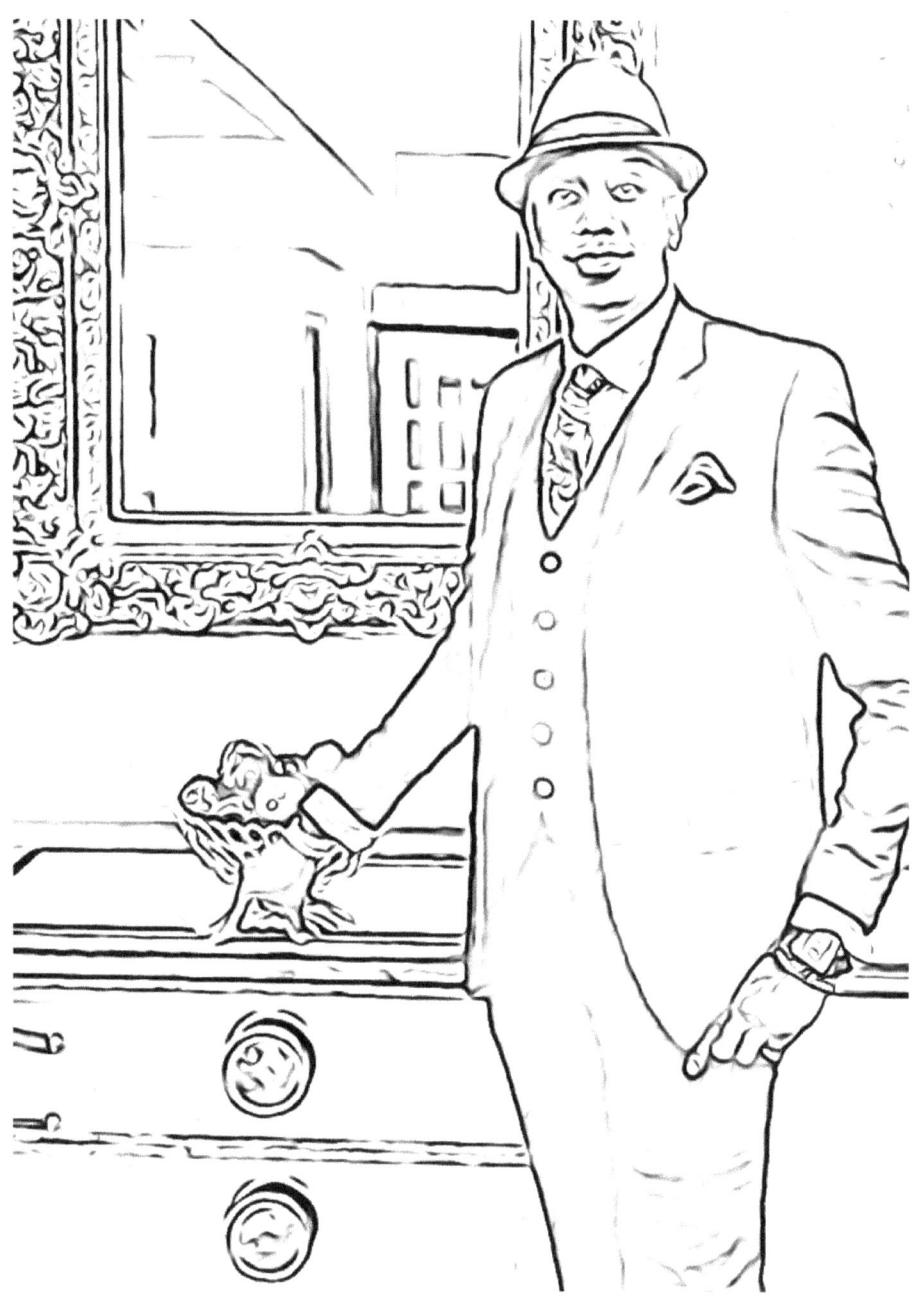

Who do you know outside of your home that you trust to give you advice if something was bothering you?

1. Who is the person you trust with the things that upset you emotionally ?

2. Who do you look up to outside of your family ?

3. Why do you look up to this person?

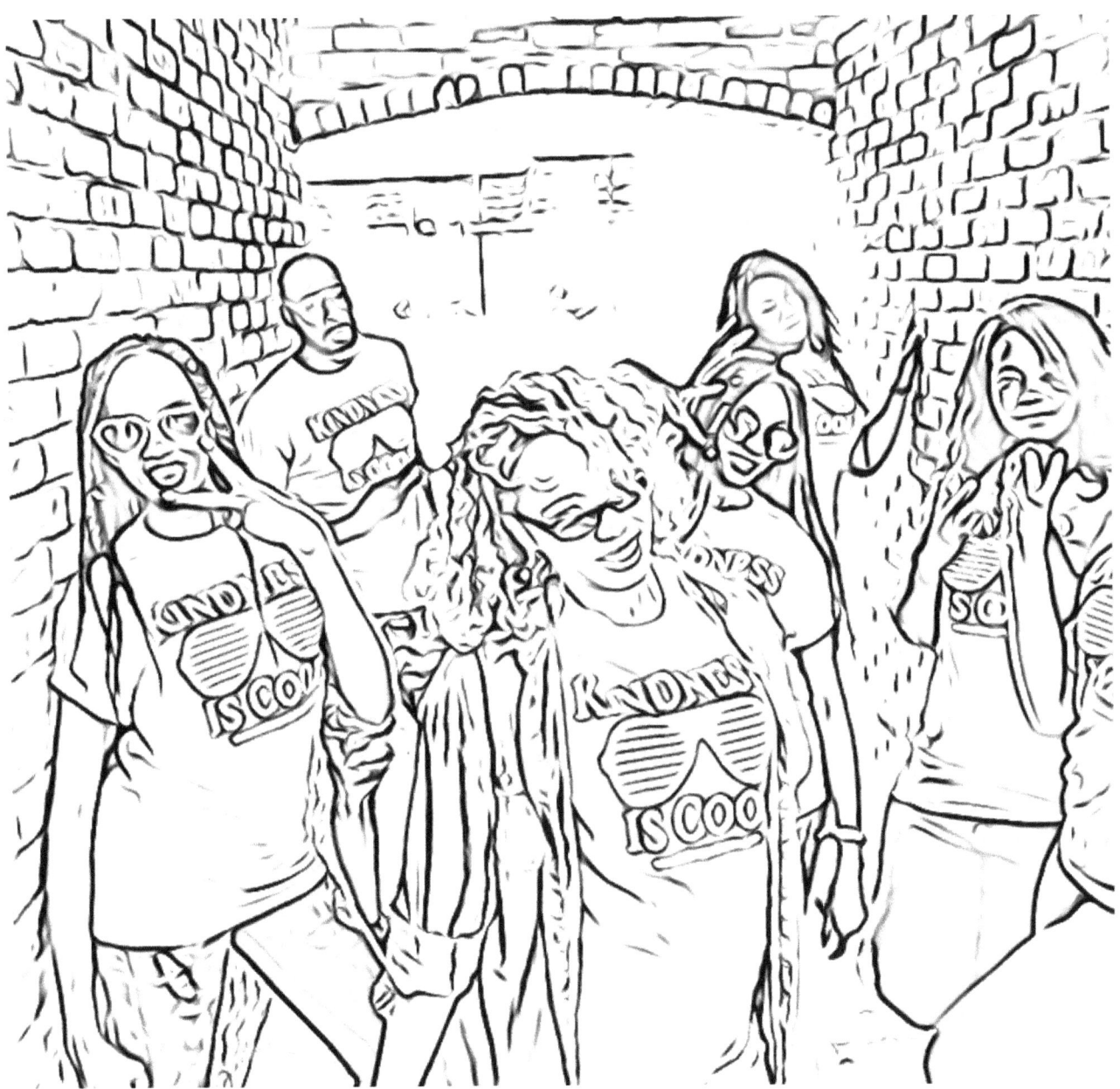

We are better together, the awareness of Bullying improves because we all get involved. Kindness is an approach not a reaction to bullying.

1. What is the most hurtful thing about bullying that you wish would stop today?

2. Do you have any classmates that help to stop bullying?

3. What does your classmate do that helps stop bullying ?

4. Write them a thank you note about how you appreciate how they help to stop bullying.

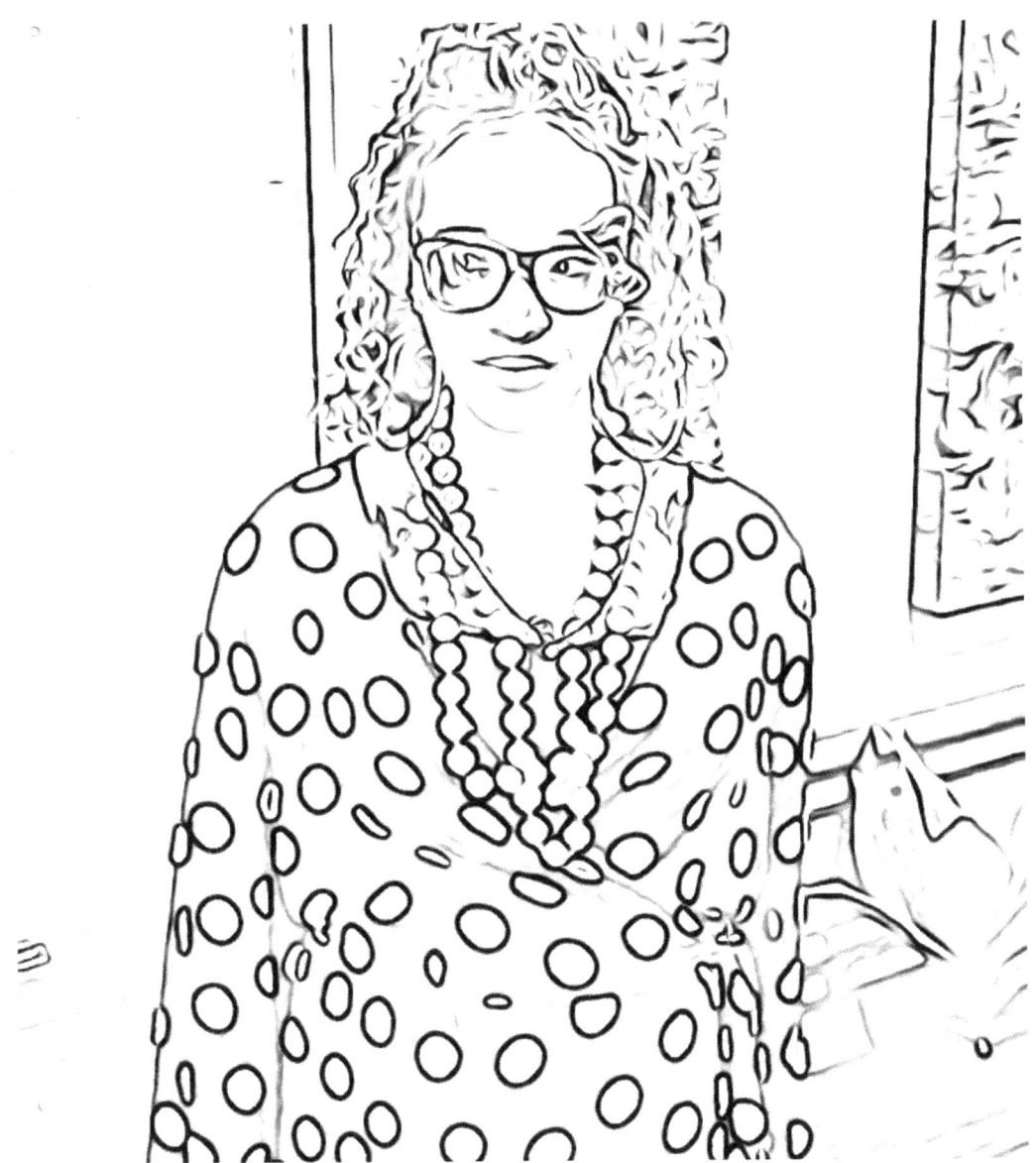

The Internet, Apps and TV provide people for us to follow, but who should we admire?

1. Who's the person or group you follow on social media outlets like Facebook, YouTube, Snapchat or Instagram the most?

2. Who do you admire that you know and why do you admire them?

3. Ask yourself how does the person I admire treat people?

4. What should I admire about people?

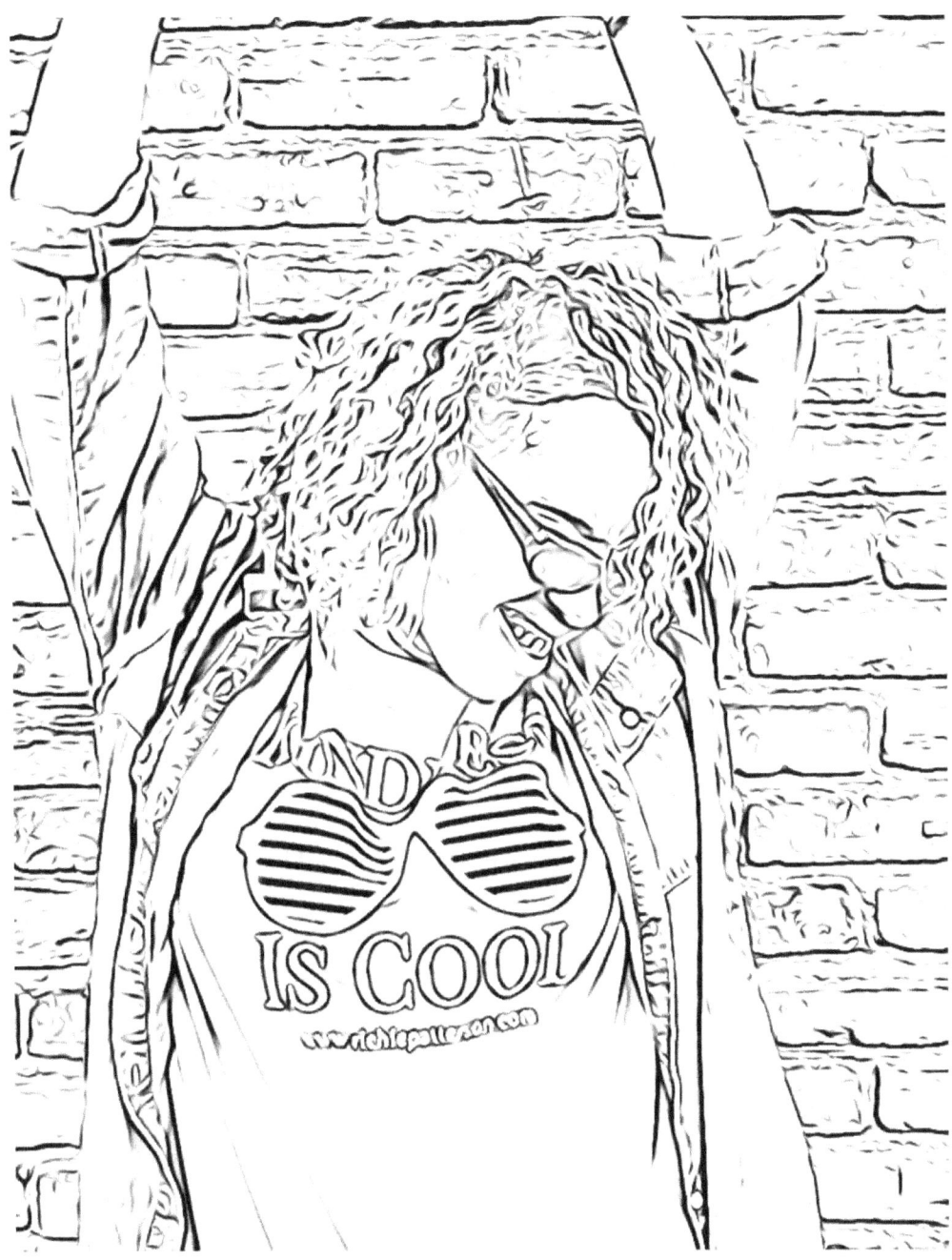

Do you admire those who get attention? Do you admire clothes and swag? How we treat people positively is something we should admire. Look up to people who are nice to other people.

1. How important is it to have swag?

2. How important is it to be accepted by your peers or classmates ?

3. How important is it that your parent or guardian be proud of your behavior?

4. Does swag help you to focus on things that are difficult to accomplish?

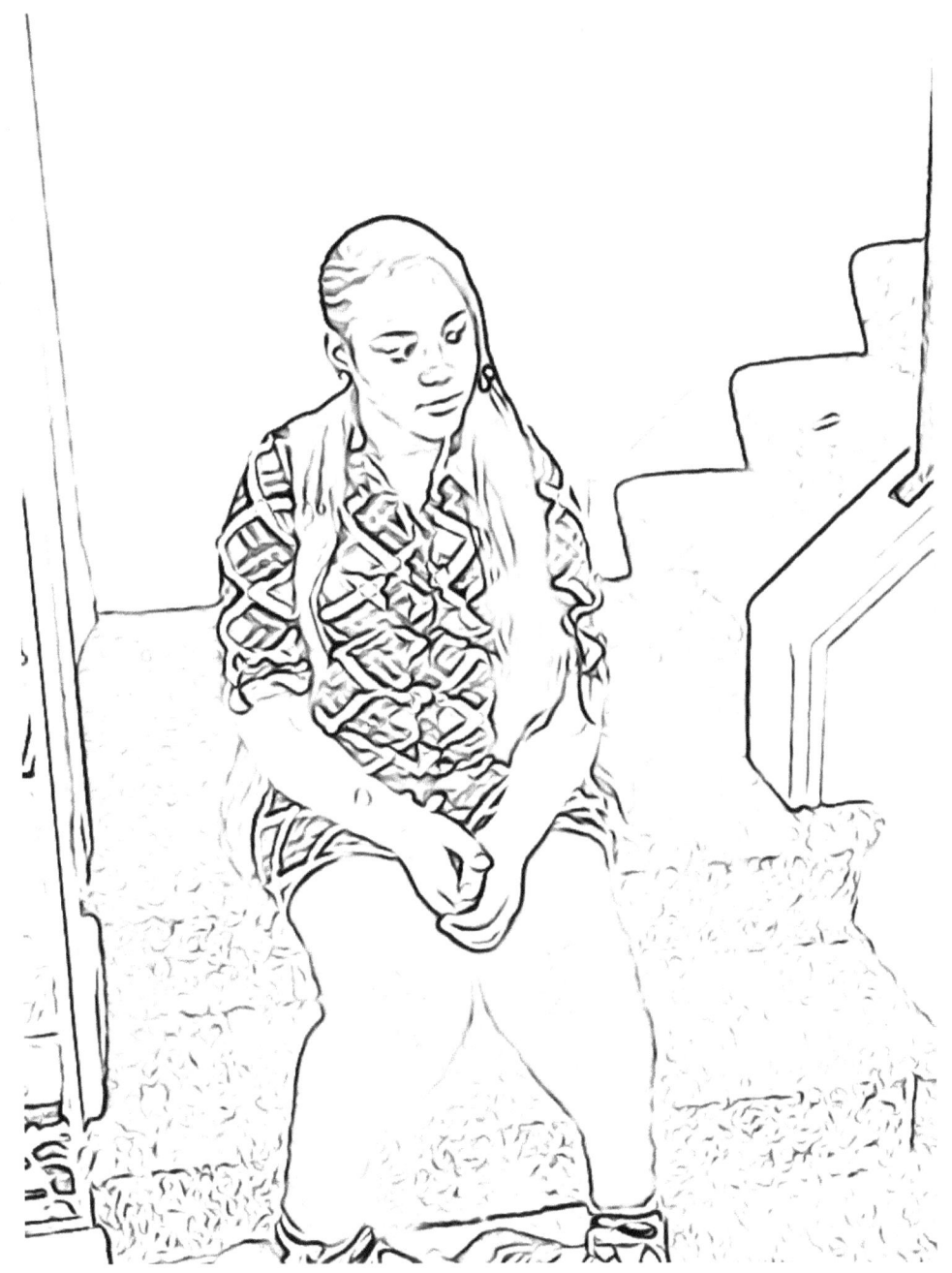

    You are beautiful not because of Swag or how people see you. Your beauty exist because God created you beautiful and you have great worth. You are not an accident but you were and are wonderfully made by God.

1. Ask yourself who on earth is 100% just like me?

2. Look in the mirror or point to yourself and say I was created with a purpose.

3. What unique talent or skill do you possess?

4. What's the one thing you would never change about yourself?

Kindness Is Cool (No More Bullying)

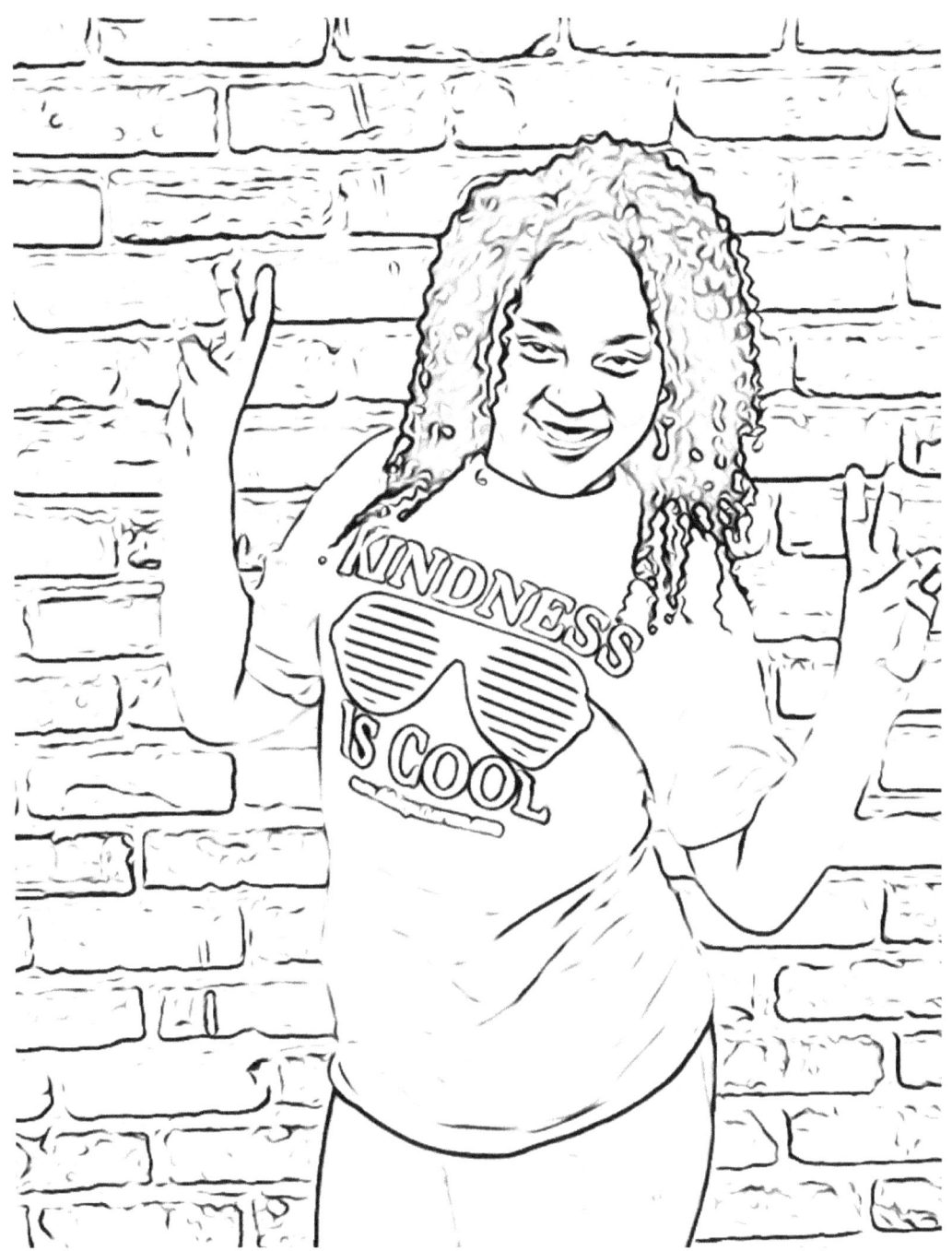

No one else in the world is 100% like you. Understand the Kindness you show to others like a fingerprint expresses your uniqueness.

1. What is a compliment?

2. How do you give a compliment to a person?

3. When was the last time you gave a compliment and what was the compliment?

4. In your opinion how do people feel emotionally when you compliment them?

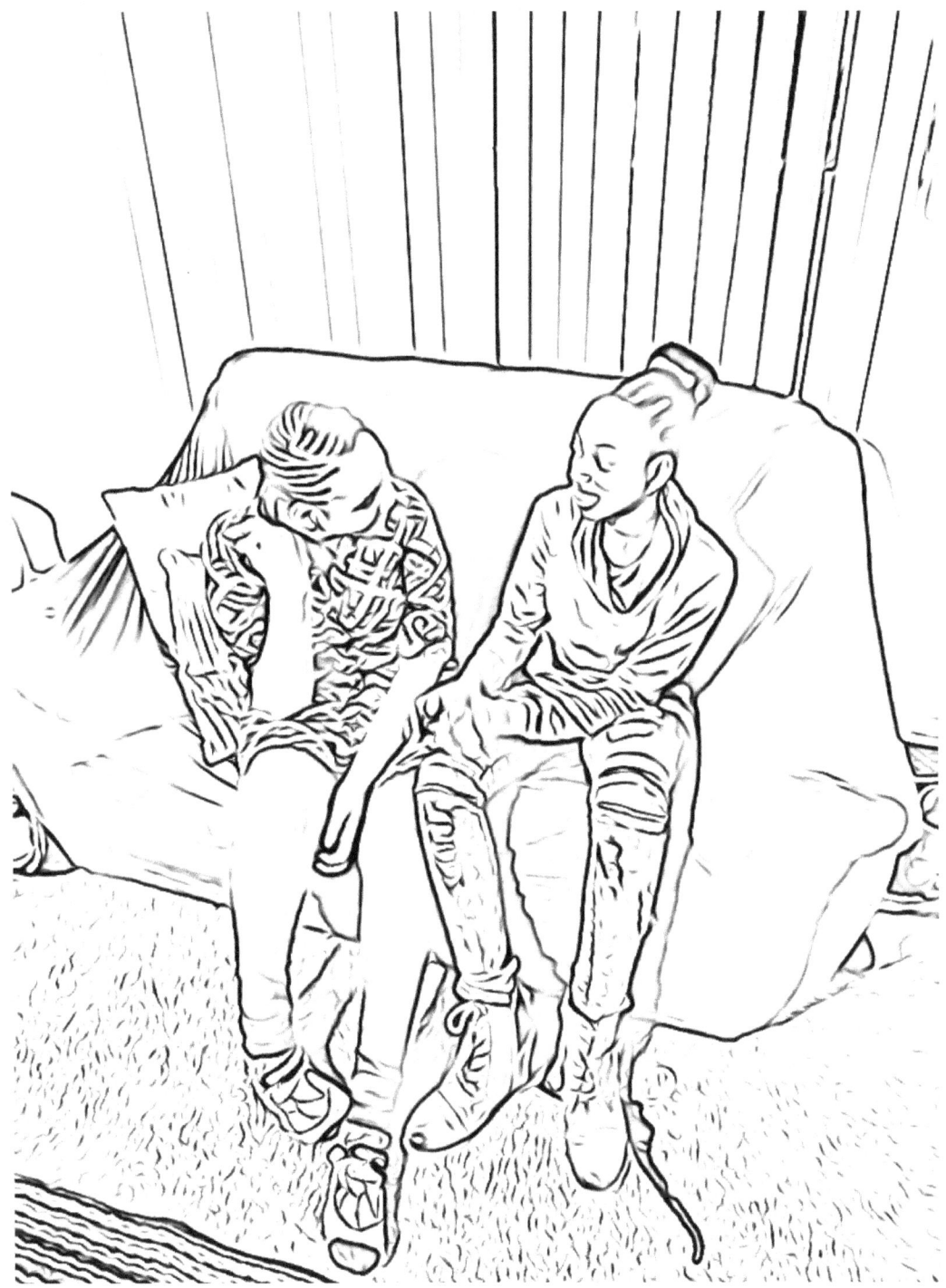

Do you use your words to compliment people or to tear them down. Always understand your words can impact people emotionally.

1. What word would best describe how you talk to people?

2. What words do you use when you're angry?

3. What do you say to yourself when you are upset with someone?

4. Who do you reach out to when you have disagreements with other peers or students?

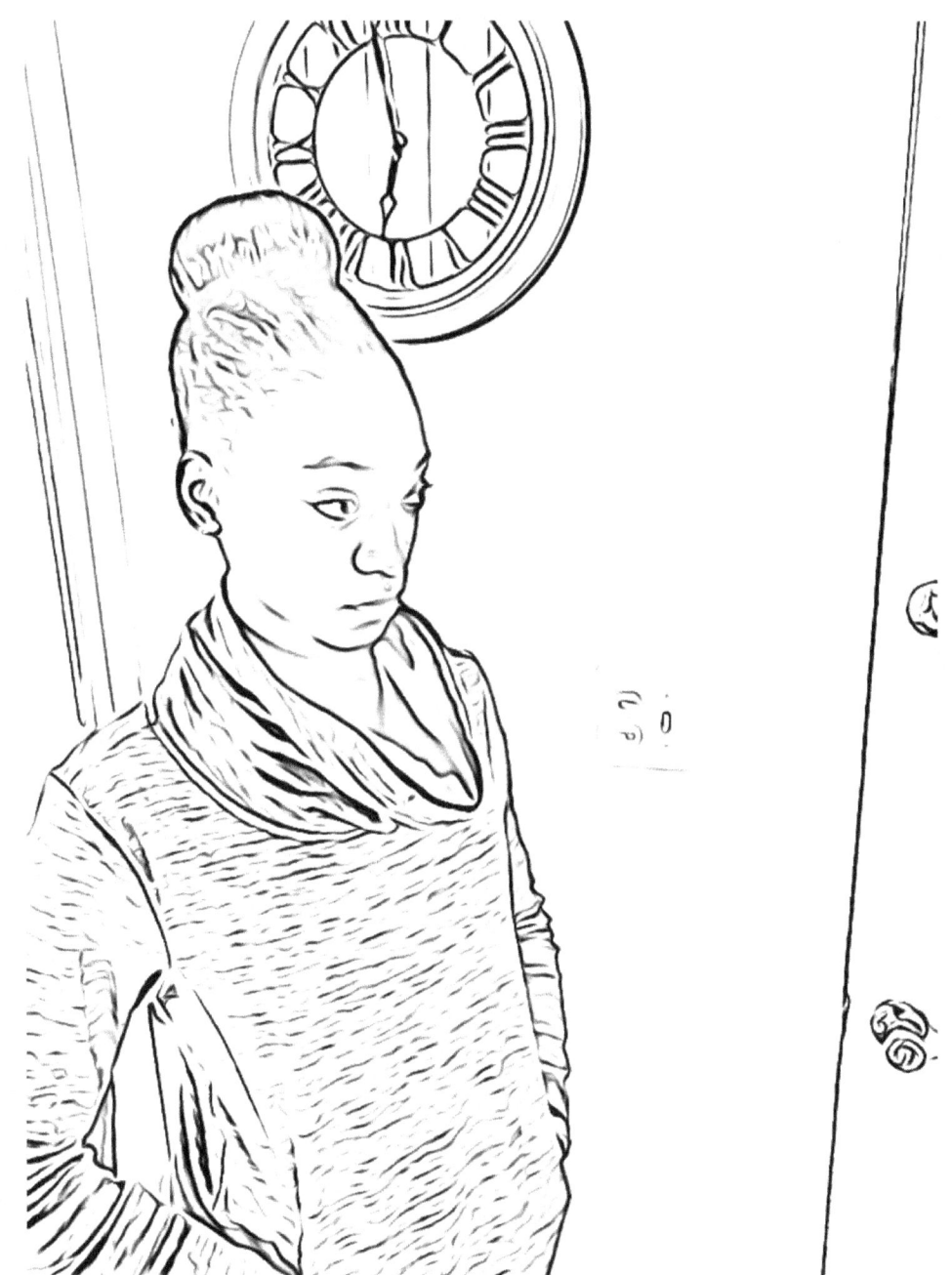

When people say mean things your feelings are impacted. Feelings unfortunately should not just be overlooked but require attention. It's ok to ask people about how they deal with feelings so you can overcome your own feelings.

1. What should I say to myself to feel better?

2. Who can help me with overcoming how I feel?

3. List the people or a person you trust in your family?

4. Name one staff member here or teacher you feel comfortable enough to talk to?

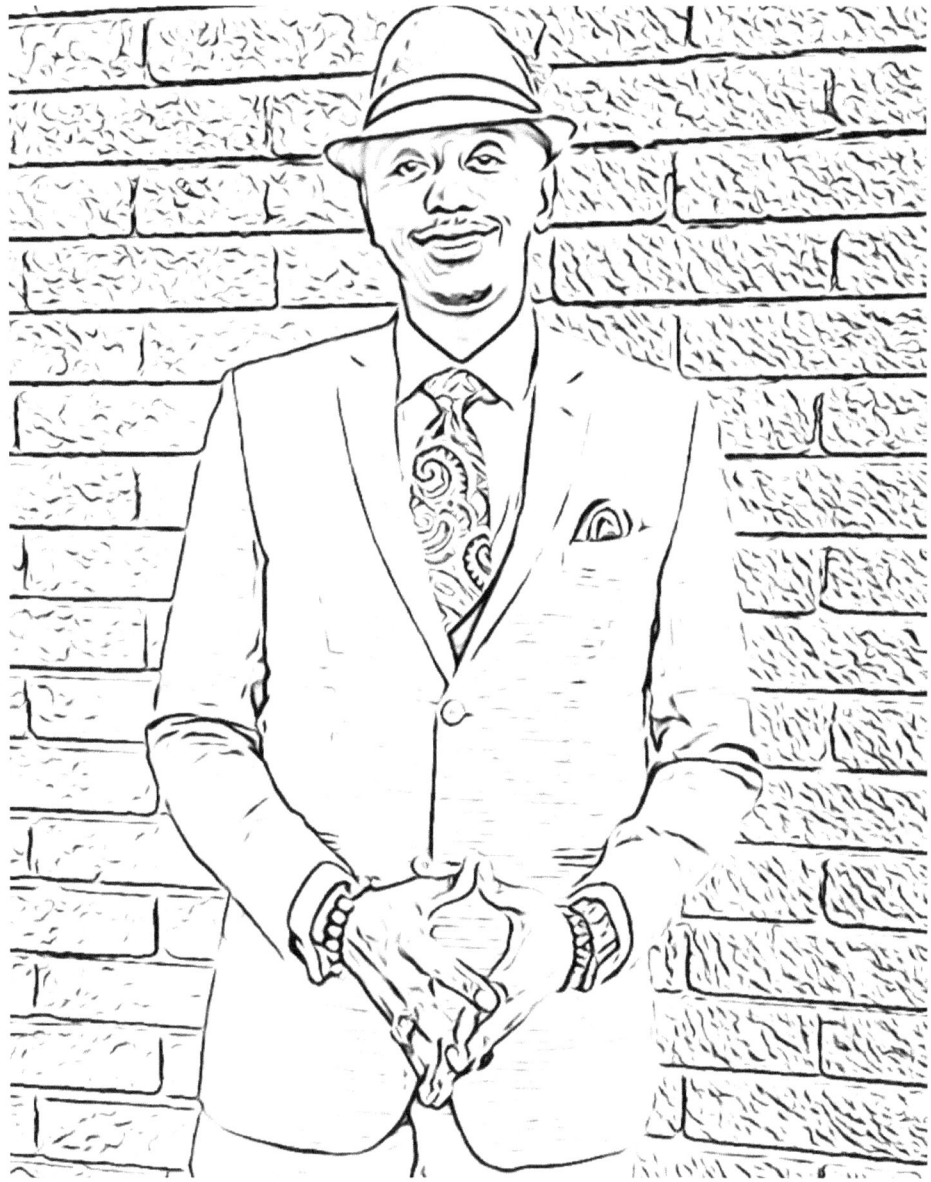

Always Remember there are people right around you that are willing to help you with questions about how you feel or any general concern. Feel free to talk to reach out to a trusted source.

1. How can we make it easier for you to come to us when you have a question about a Bullying situation?

2. What is the most common way people are bullied?

3. What are some uncommon ways people are bullied?

4. What suggestions do you have to prevent or stop bullying?

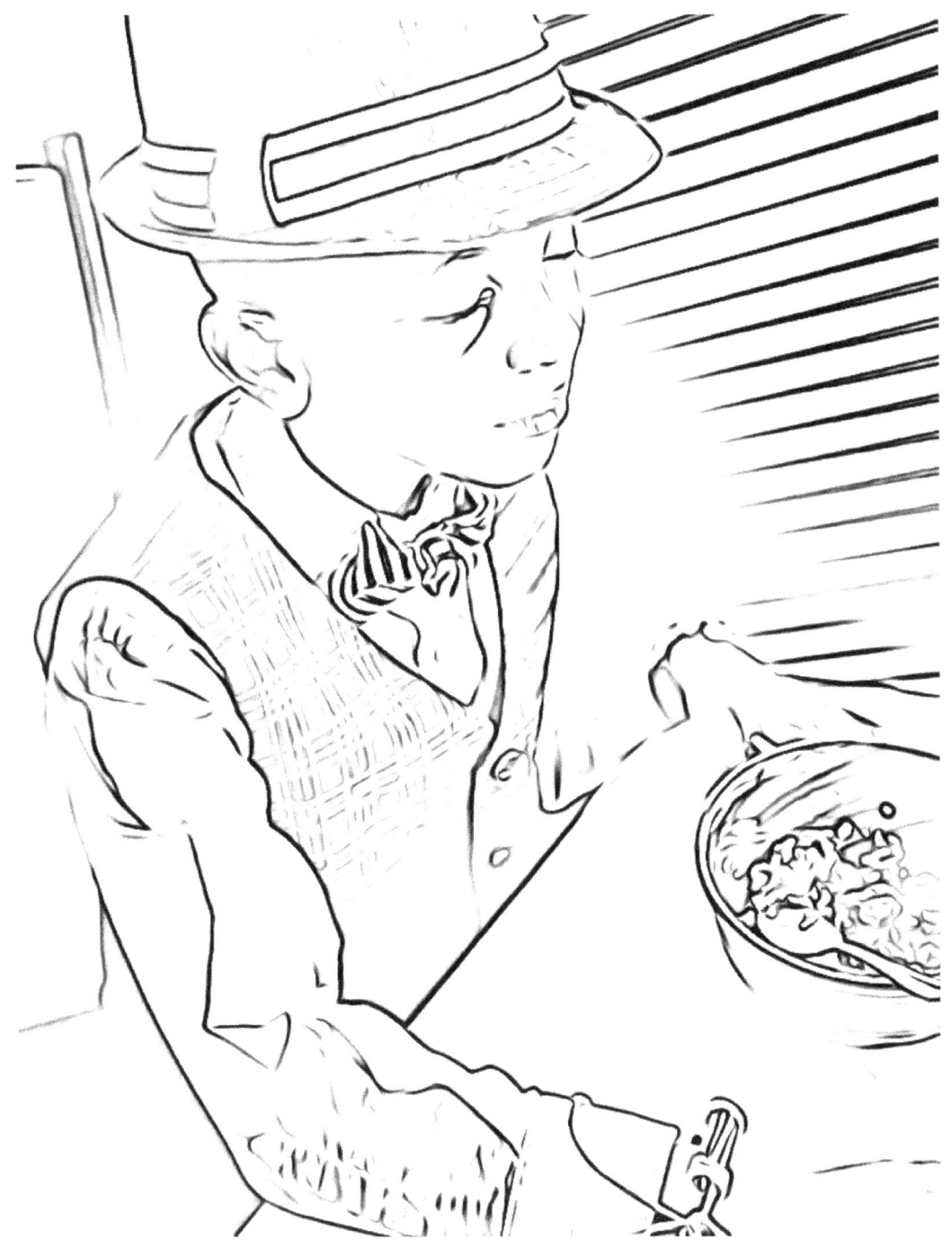

Just like you can pray over your food, you can pray and ask God to help you with your feelings Amen.

1. Who or what helps you feel better when you are sad, angry or disappointed?

2. What do you watch on TV or what app do you use that inspires you?

3. Name one person who gives you advice about how to deal with your feelings?

4. Name one feeling you overcame in the past and how did you overcome that feeling?

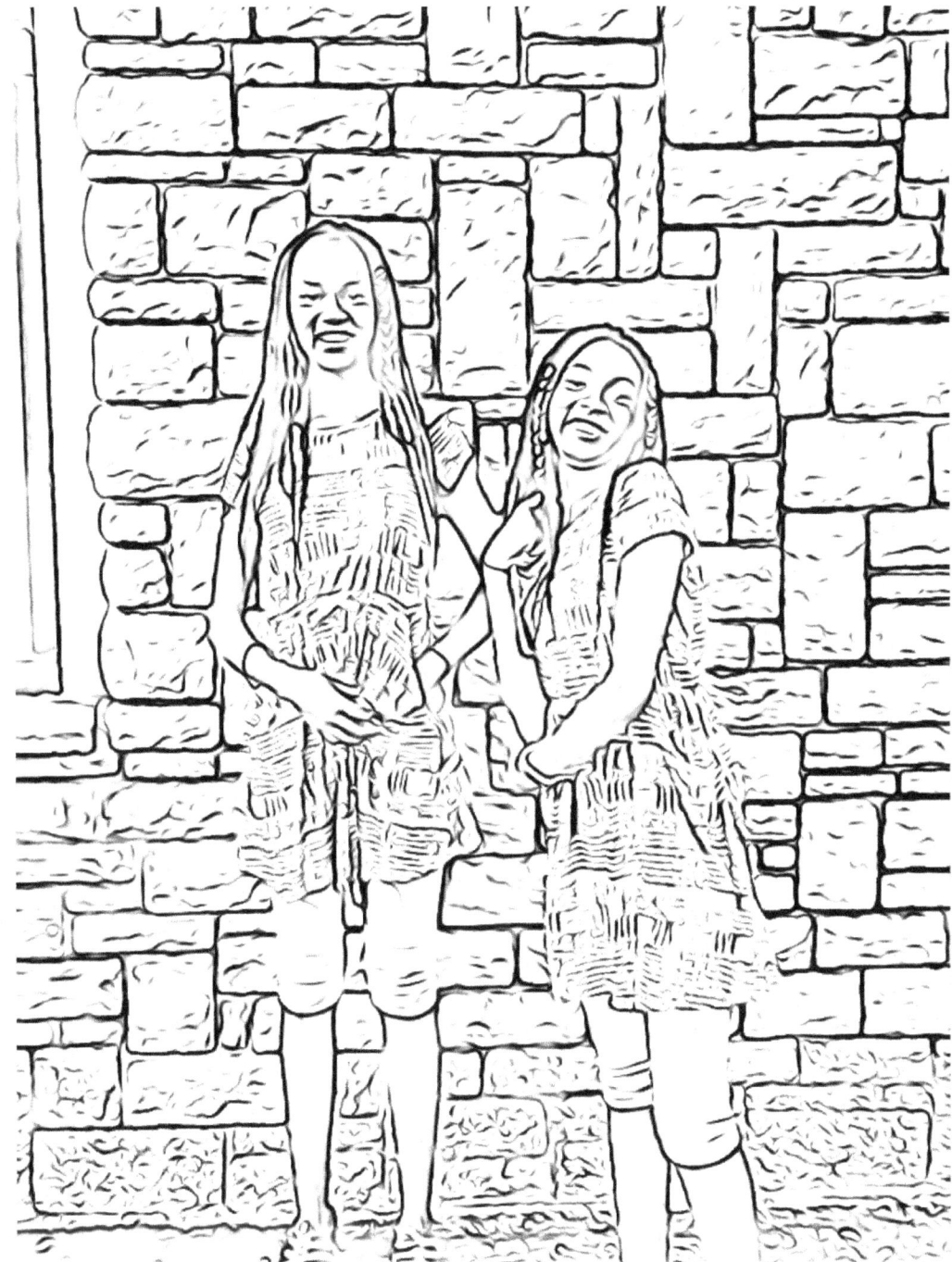

When you are dressed nice you feel nice, and in that moment you say to yourself I'm handsome or pretty. Dress yourself with Kind words that remind you of what's good about yourself and life.

1. What was the last Kind thing you said to yourself?

2. Do you remember the last Kind words that were said to you and when were they said?

3. In this moment say something Kind about yourself, name one thing that's Kind about you?

4. In this moment say something Kind to the person next to you or next person you're near in the next few hours.

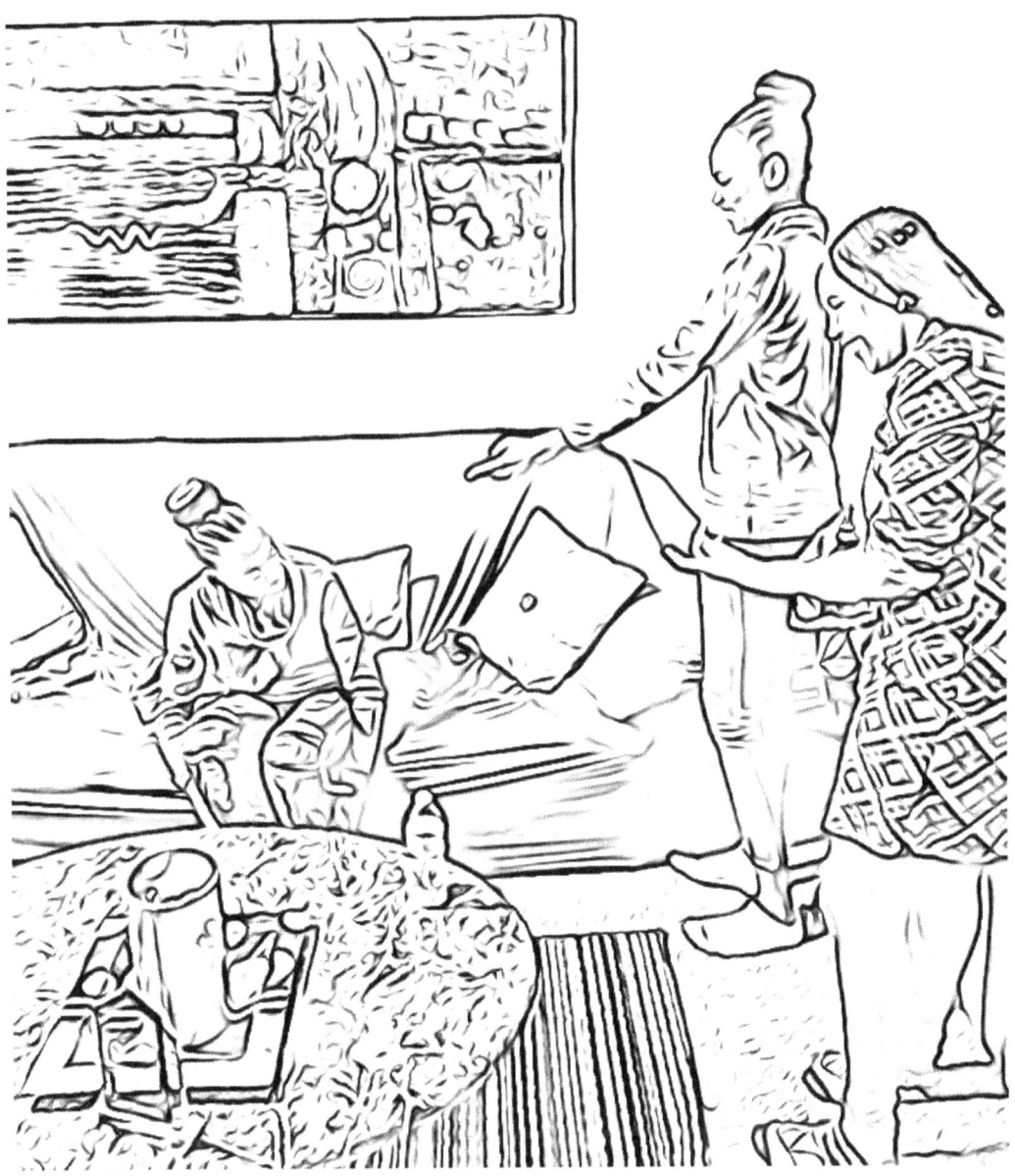

With all that you say to yourself, people can be insensitive at times and you can feel picked on. Understand how people see you does not define your worth or value.

1. When a person says negative things to you, remind yourself that you have value beyond their negativity.

2. Why do people pick on other people?

3. How do I know if I'm the person who's picking on someone else?

4. When I talk to a teacher, family member, peer or counselor should I tell them about what was said or done that was hurtful?

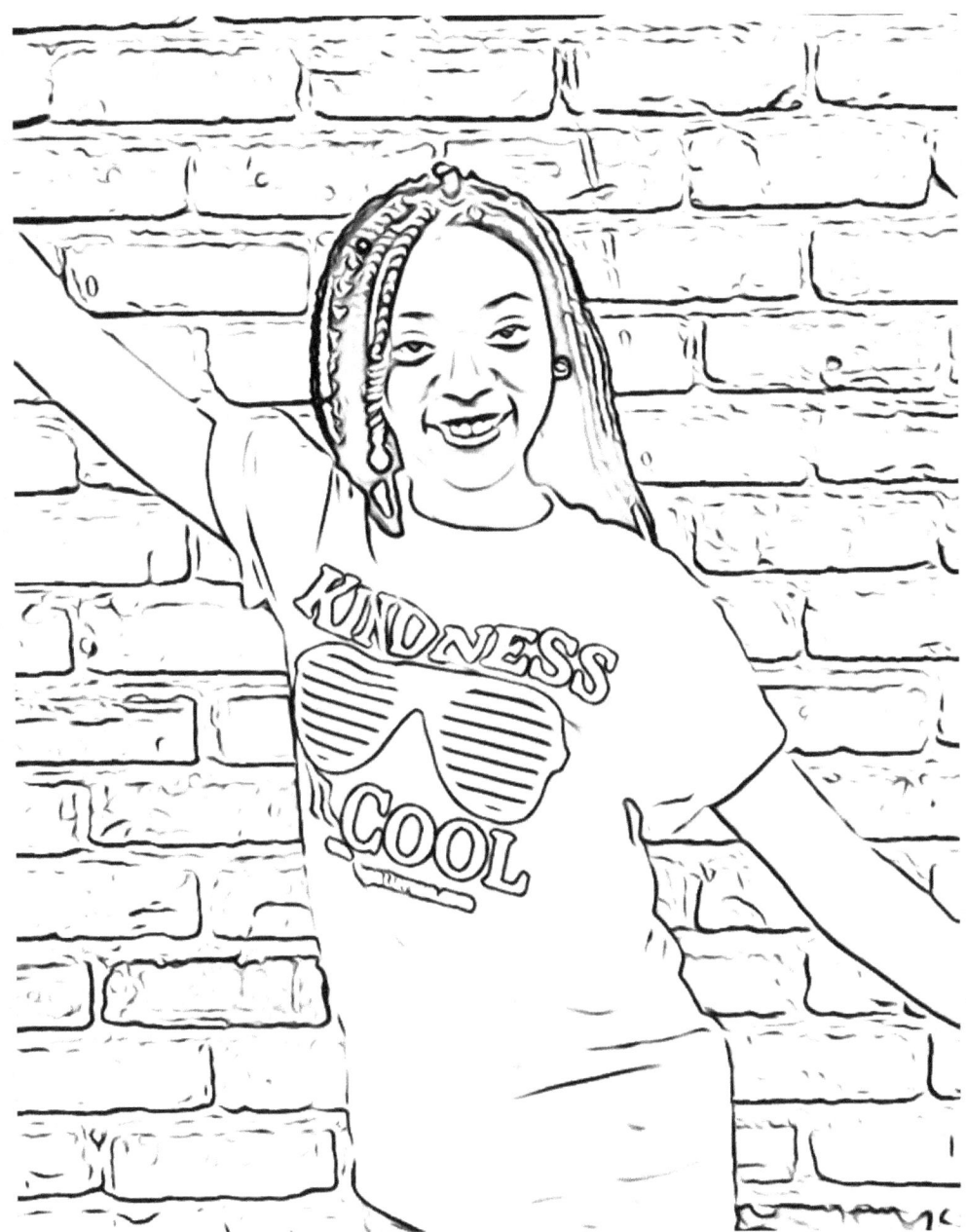

You are still that same beautiful person that you were when you woke up this morning. Kindness is always more powerful than negativity. See your inner beauty more than those who seek to bully you.

1. List what you love the most about your life?

2. Take 30 seconds and think about the people you love and how they make you feel good about yourself?

3. Smile at someone in the room and say you are not my enemy, but you are my friend.

4. In this moment think about how you can be Kind to a person who maybe wasn't Kind to you.

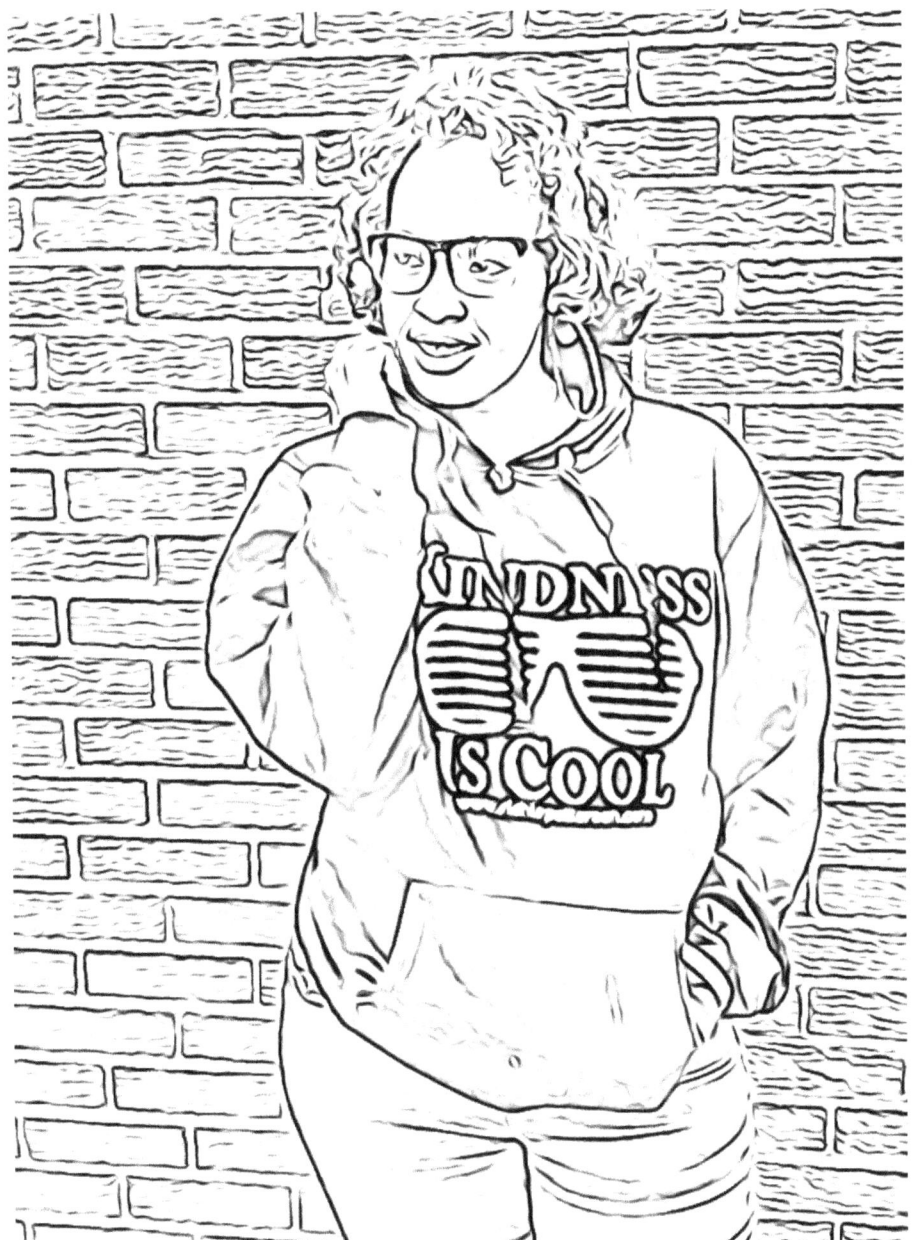

There are people who are just Cool because of their personality. The coolest thing you can do when a Bullying situation arises is to reach out to trusted sources for help.

Kindness Is Cool (No More Bullying)

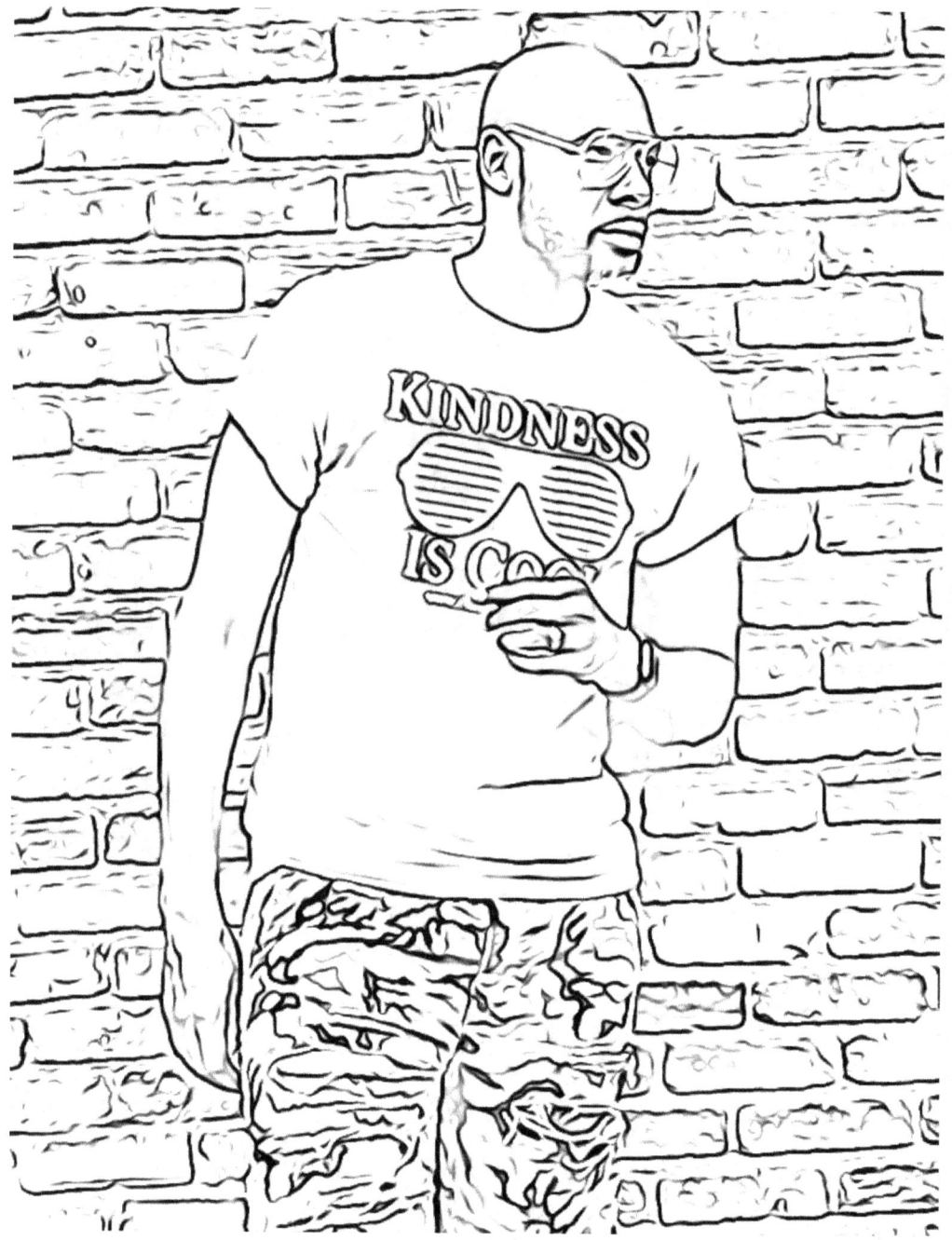

Dad may not be around when yourself or someone else is being bullied but it's ok to reach out for help. Asking for help is Cool and it's Kind.

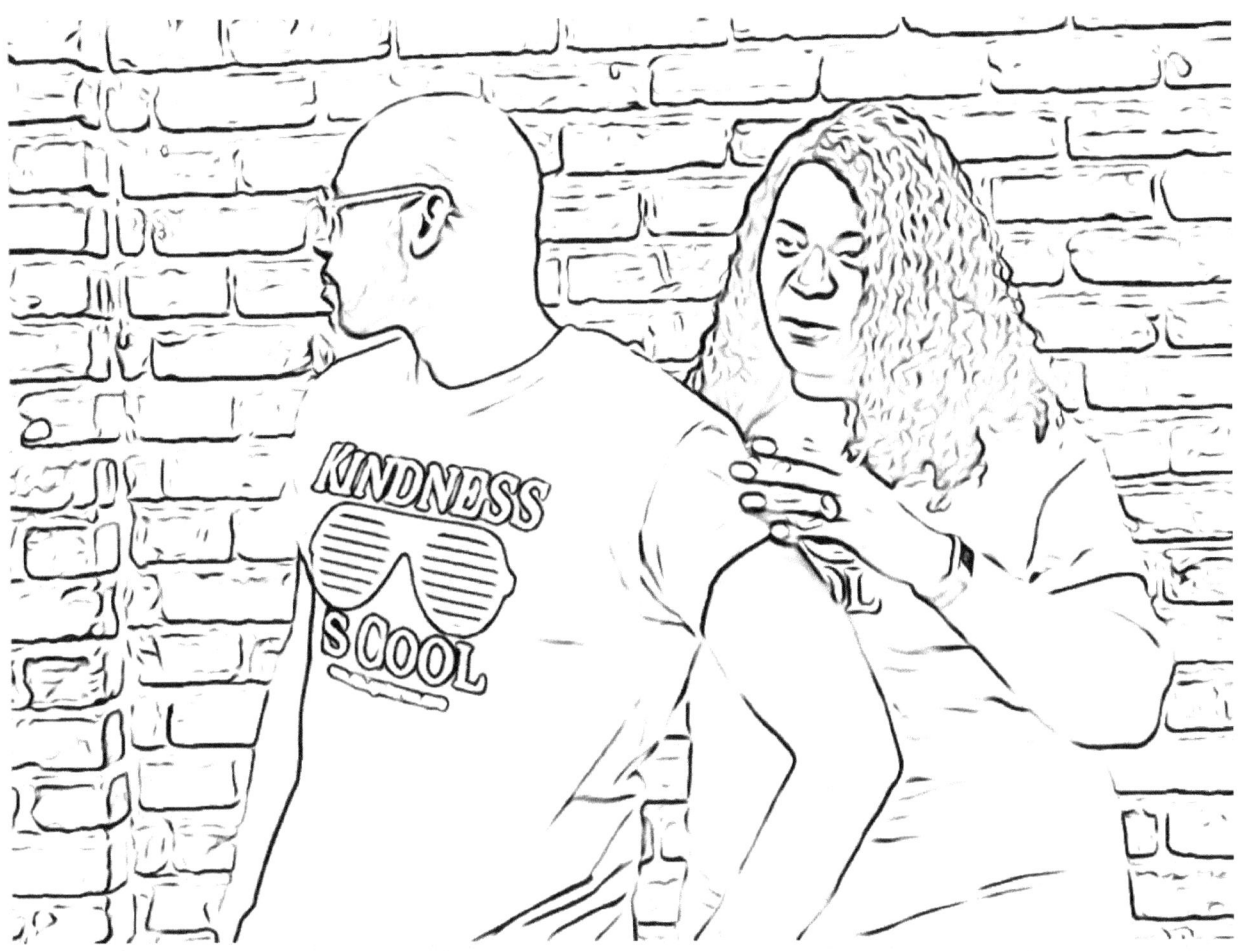

Mom supports Dad but how do I support a person who I believe is being bullied?

Kindness Is Cool (No More Bullying)

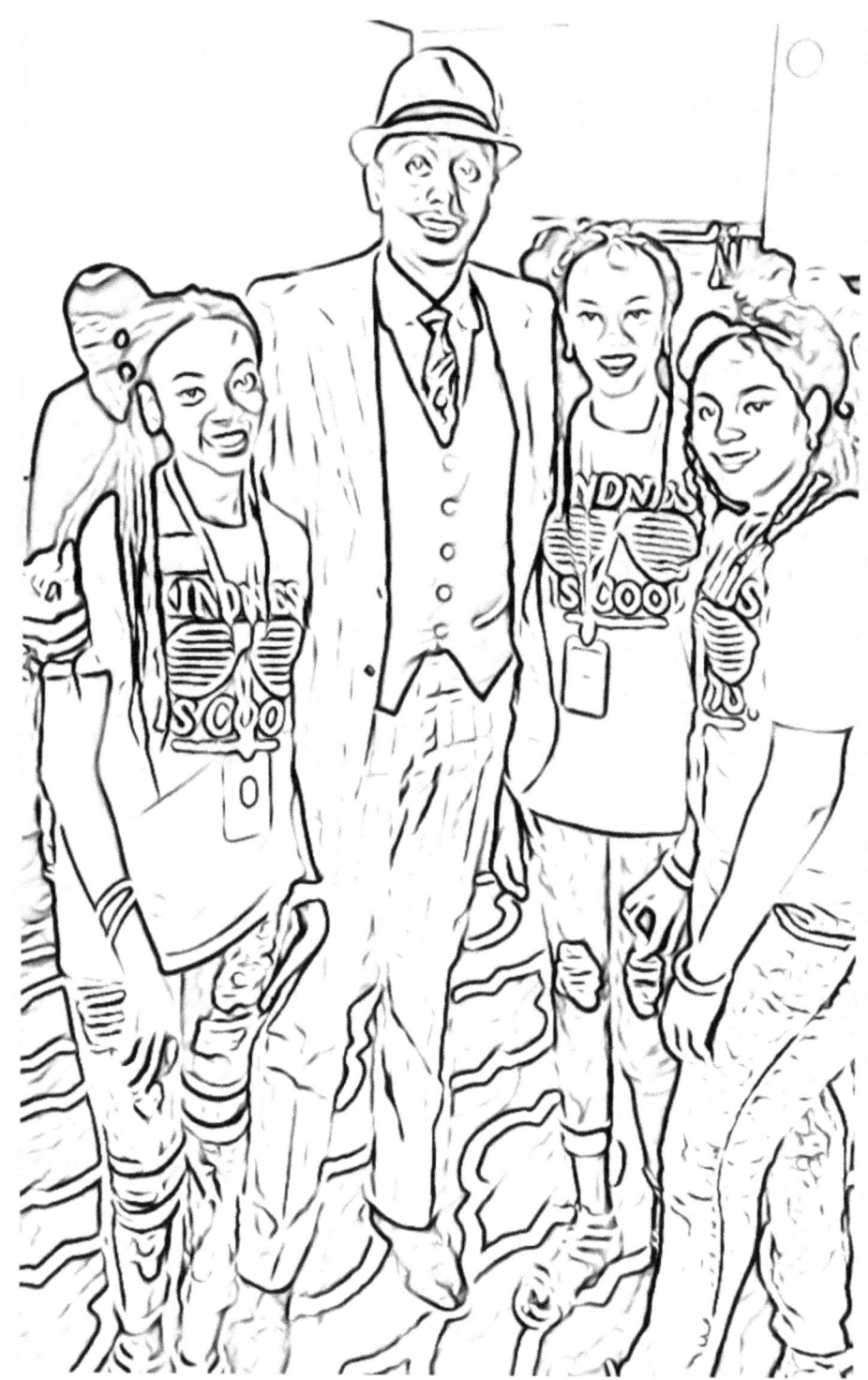

Kindness is a group effort and we all play a part to stop the Bullying.

1. When is a good time to express my feelings concerning a bullying situation?

2. Should I wait before talking to my parent, teacher, counselor or trusted source?

3. What if the person I trust is not available, what should I do in that scenario?

4. Will I be punished or seen differently for talking about a bullying situation?

Kindness Is Cool (No More Bullying)

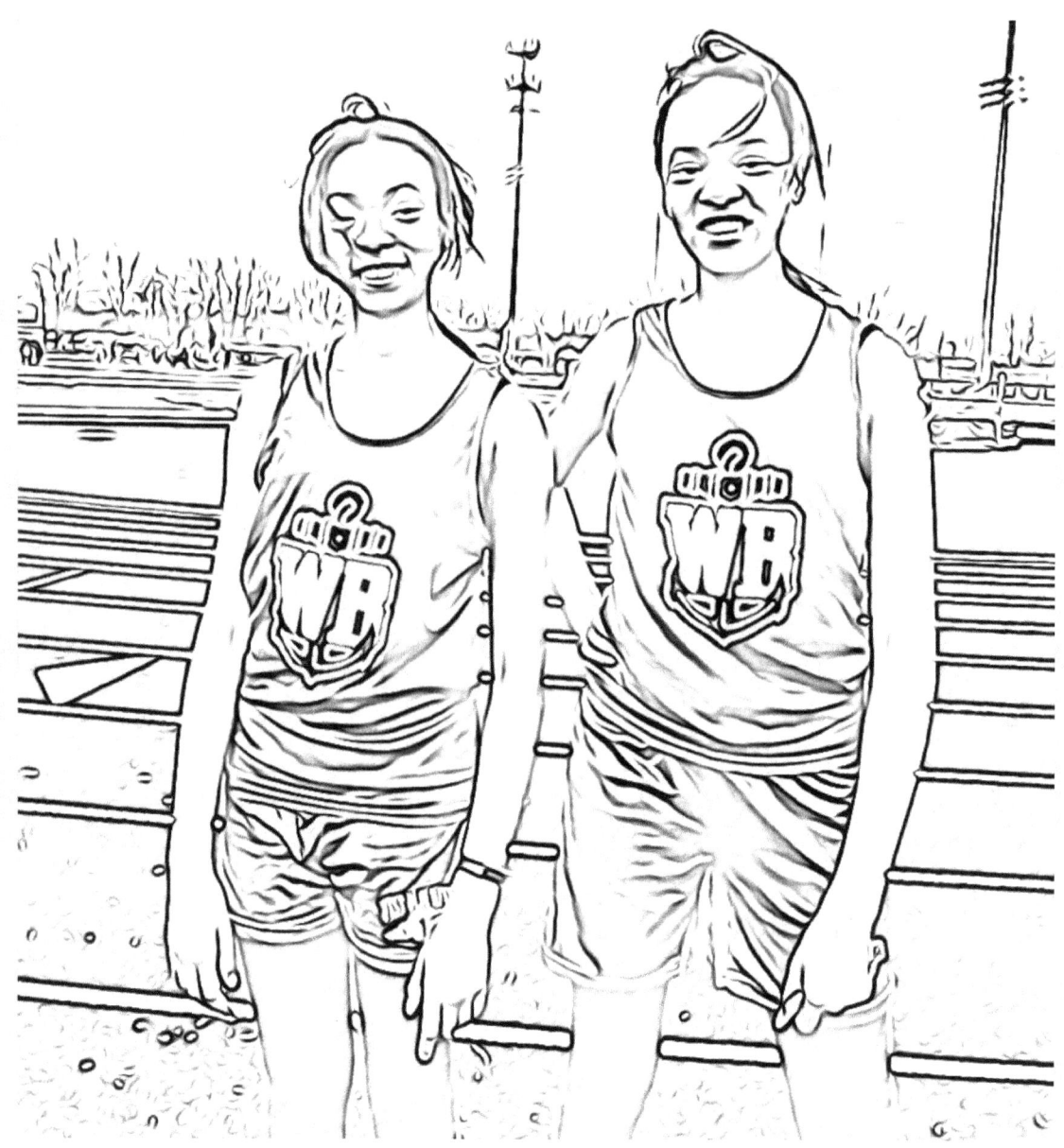

Kindness is not a quick sprint but like a marathon you have to prepare to be Kind. Kindness is not an accident but it's a choice to be nice to people.

1. What are words that could encourage people?

2. List three words that you like for people to use when they talk to you?

3. Choose one word that describes a person that you feel doesn't bully people?

4. Say to the person next to you, I Choose To think about how I can use my words to lift you up.

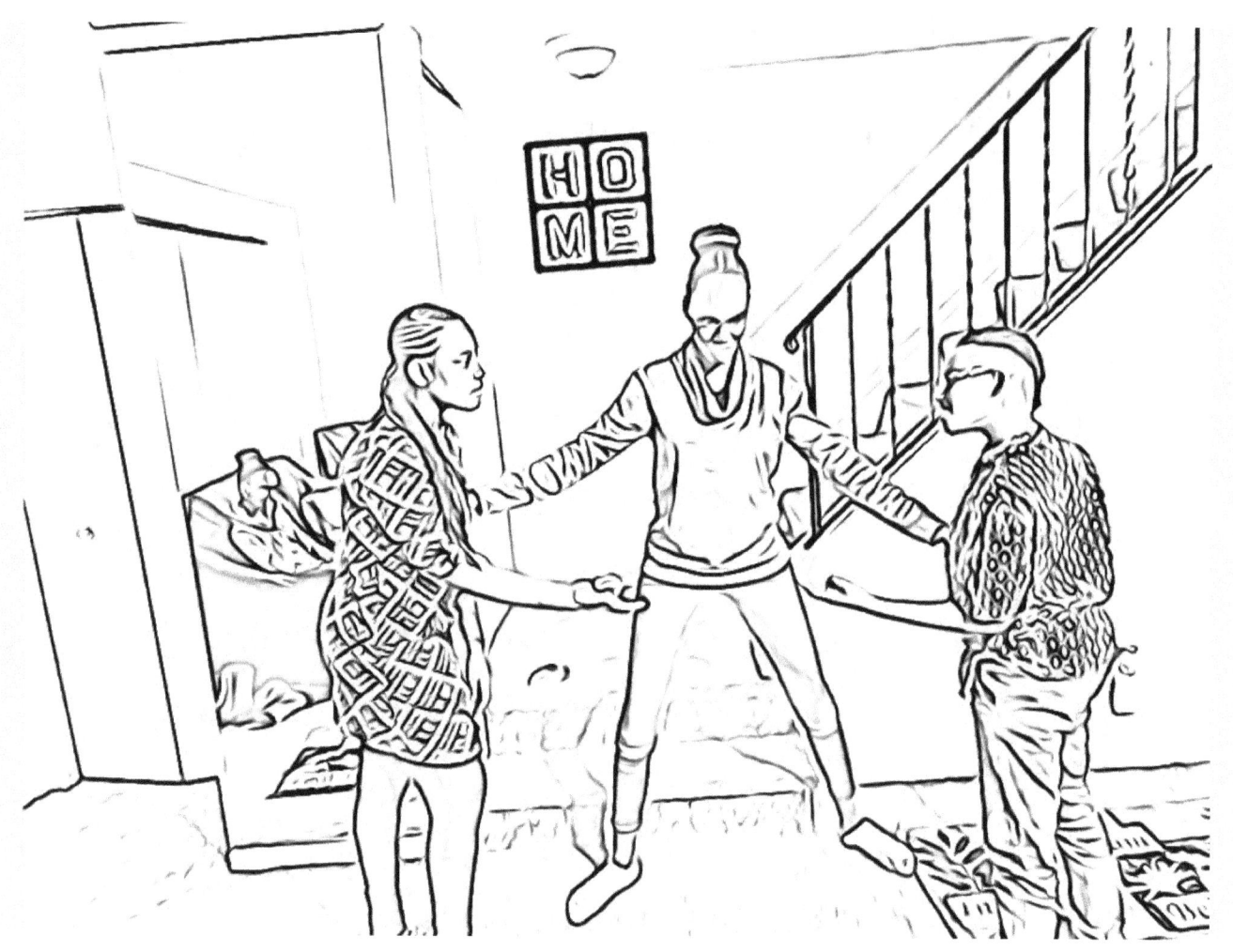

    We need people who understand how to resolve the problem. Anger without a solution will not fix anything. Kindness seeks to help the situation through compassion and reasoning with everyone that's involved.

1. Before it gets to this point, go get a teacher or staff when you hear negative words being used to hurt people's feeling.

2. It's not ok to physically use force against people, always reach out for help if a fight arises.

3. Violence is not an answer to anything. Ask other peers to get involved by not cheering the disagreement on with laughter, recording with phones or being interested in the fighting.

4. Drawing attention to a negative conversation or fight is not the way to go. When you see a hostile crowd around someone or others being negative to a person reach out for help immediately.

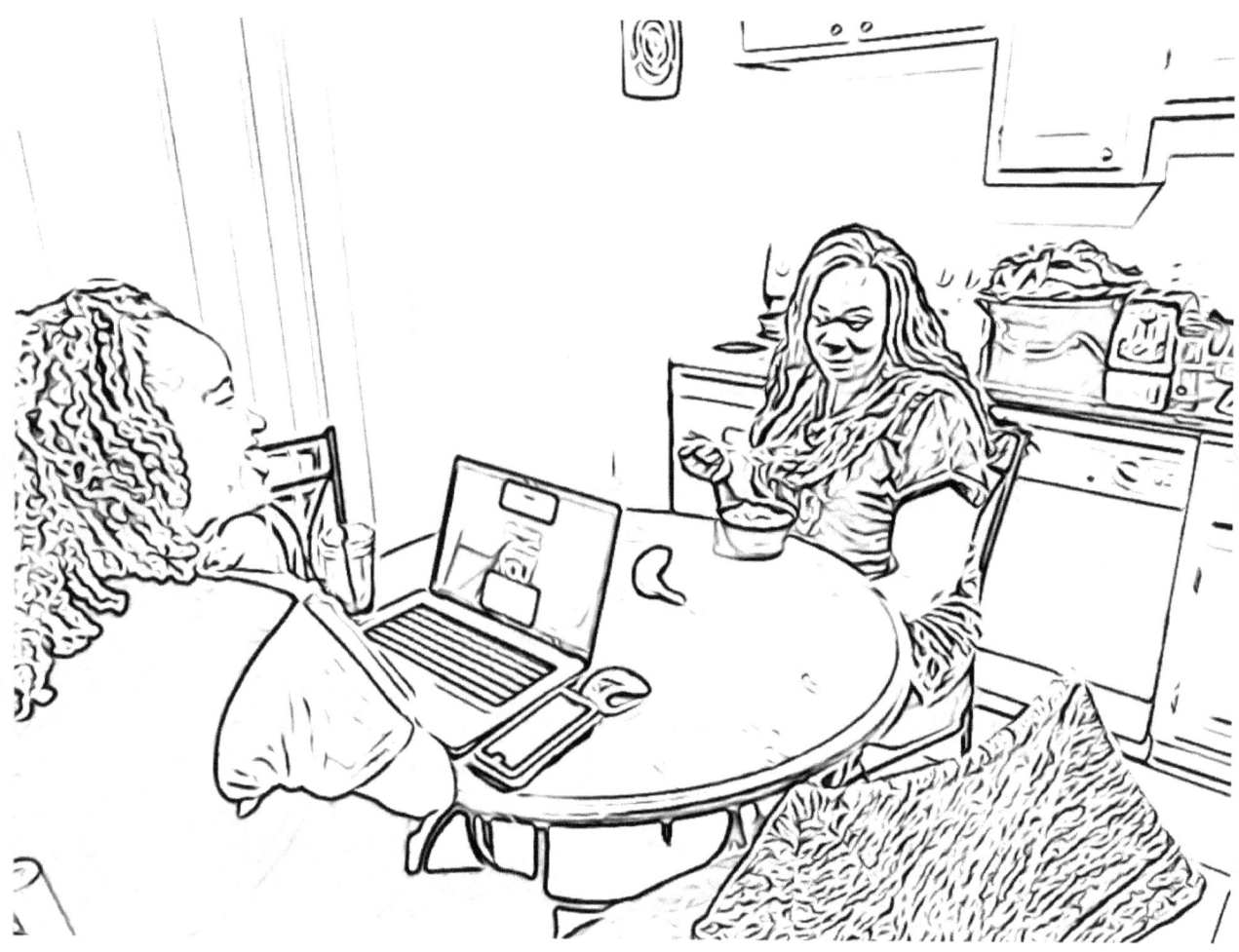

Even as Adults we play a part when a bullying situation arises. We choose to come to the table to reason together and create a solution to stop the bullying. We are not enemies of other children but we understand both parties still have value.

1. Adults should seek to reason together towards solution, we don't make the child the enemy we simply focus on the next steps to resolve the situation.

2. As an adult I am open to a counselor, teacher or a person I trust to help me and my child to get through this.

3. The organization, school or non profit has some listed resource and people who can talk the Parent and the child through a bullying situation.

4. Are you aware of what services currently exist to stop bullying in the school, city or organization?

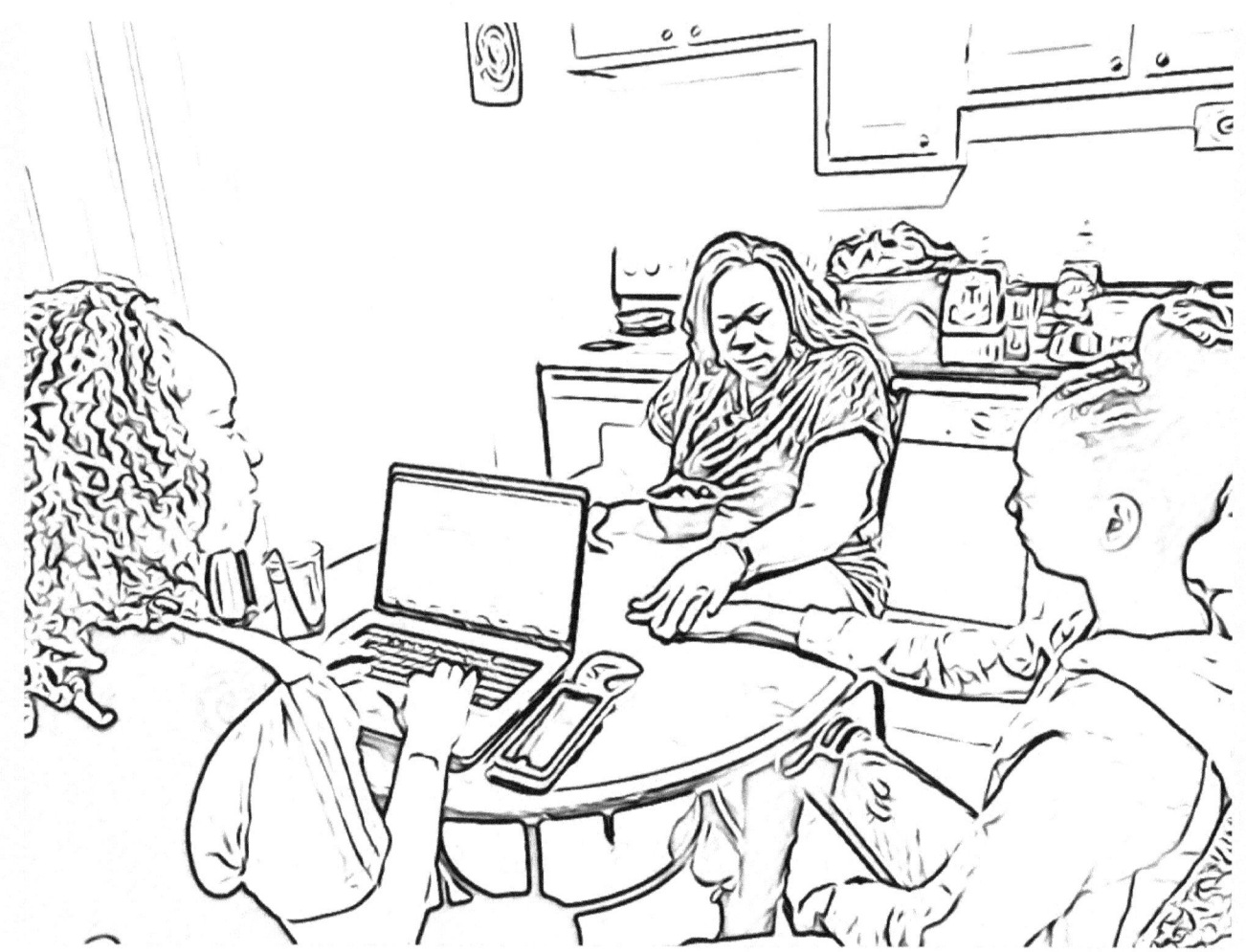

Always remember it's ok to ask for help. Never feel bad because you don't have the answer concerning a bullying situation. There's always someone you trust who can provide help and direction.

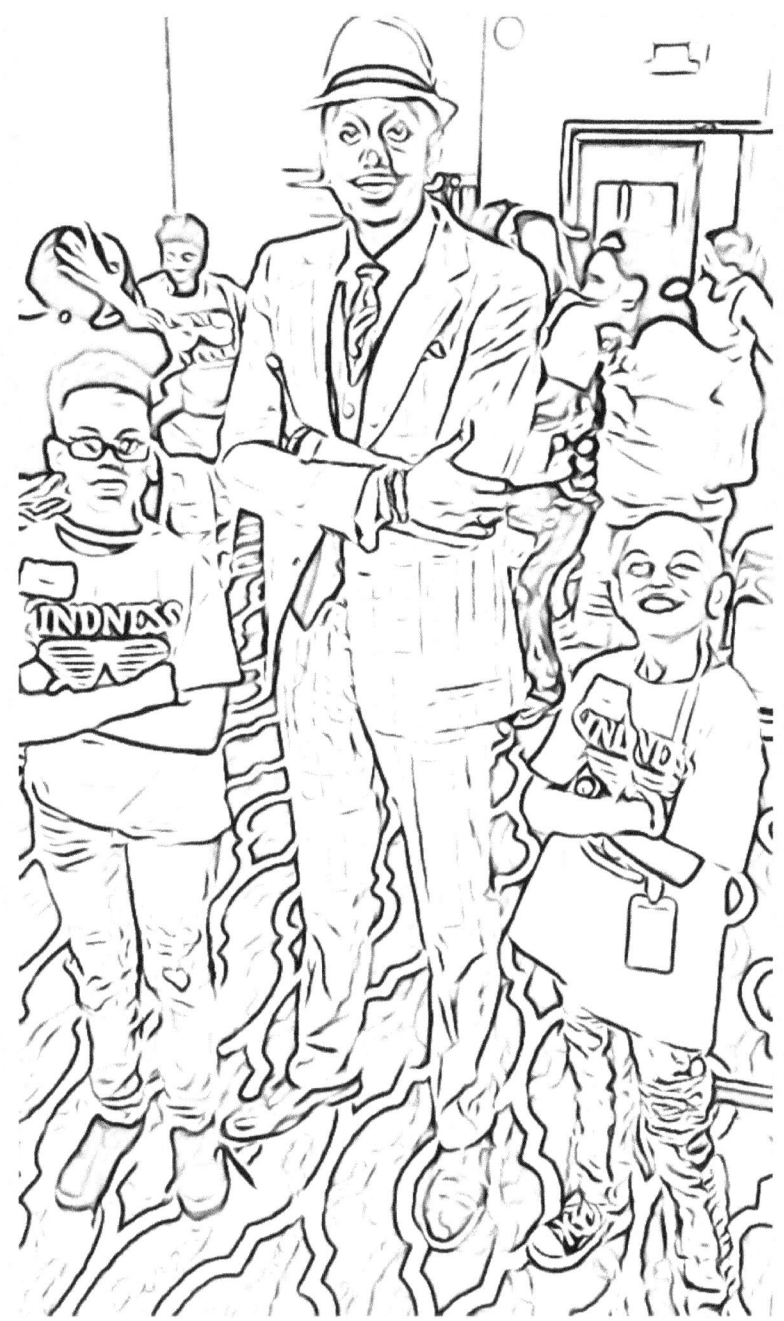

Let's make considering other people's feelings cool again. Kindness stops the bully around you and even the bully that could be in you.

1. Always consider that words are powerful and you can use them to build people up.

2. Kindness is Cool because it's how you express your uniqueness by being nice to others.

3. Kindness looks for ways to get along with people.

4. Kindness is an approach and we all know practice makes perfect so practice being considerate before anything ever happens.

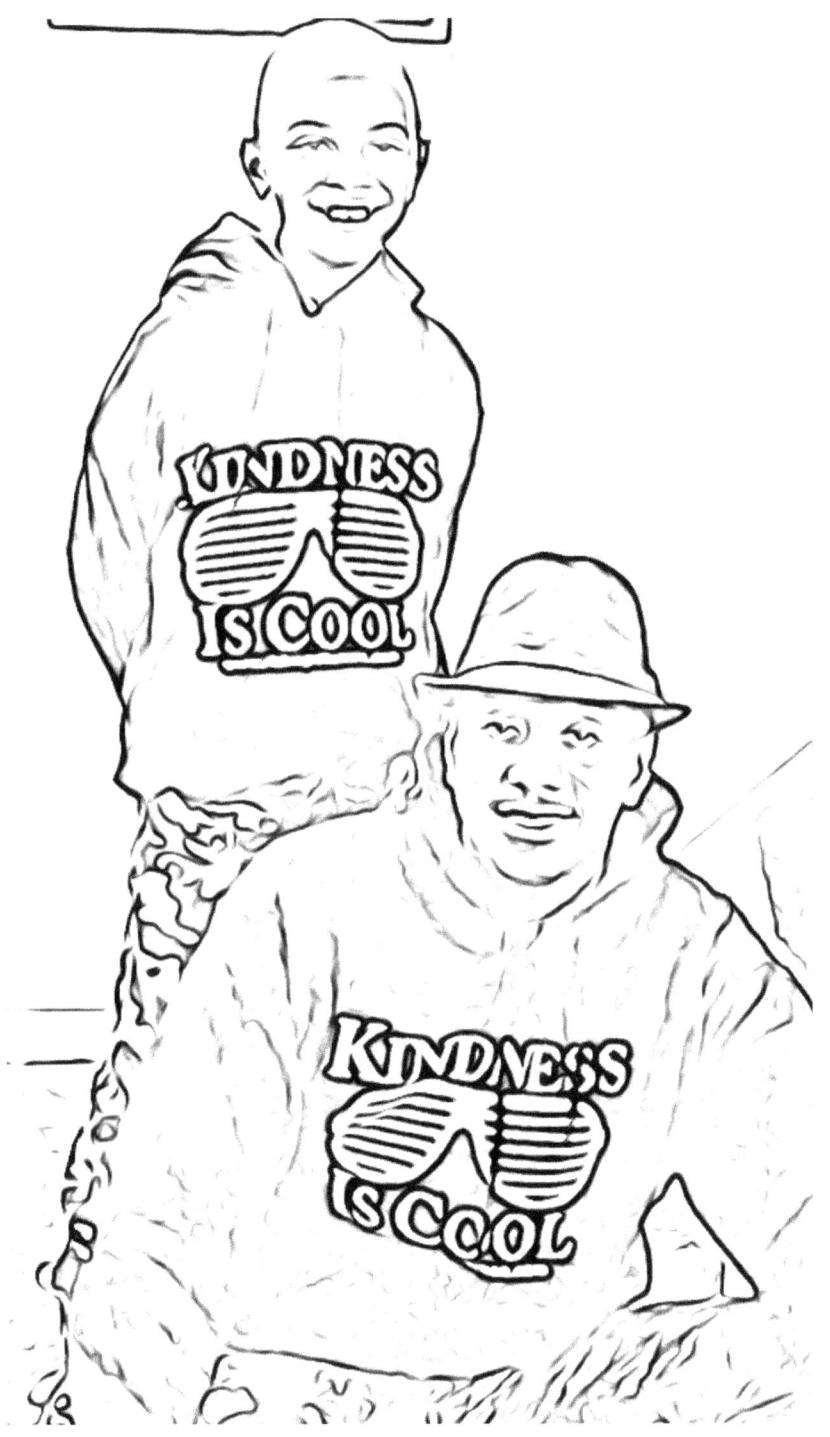

Don't let anyone tell you that Kindness is a Weakness, but understand Kindness Is Cool.

1. Remember swag can impress people, but Kindness impacts how people feel about themselves and that's powerful.

2. Strong People are considerate People

3. You were created to be Kind to others and to understand your worth and value.

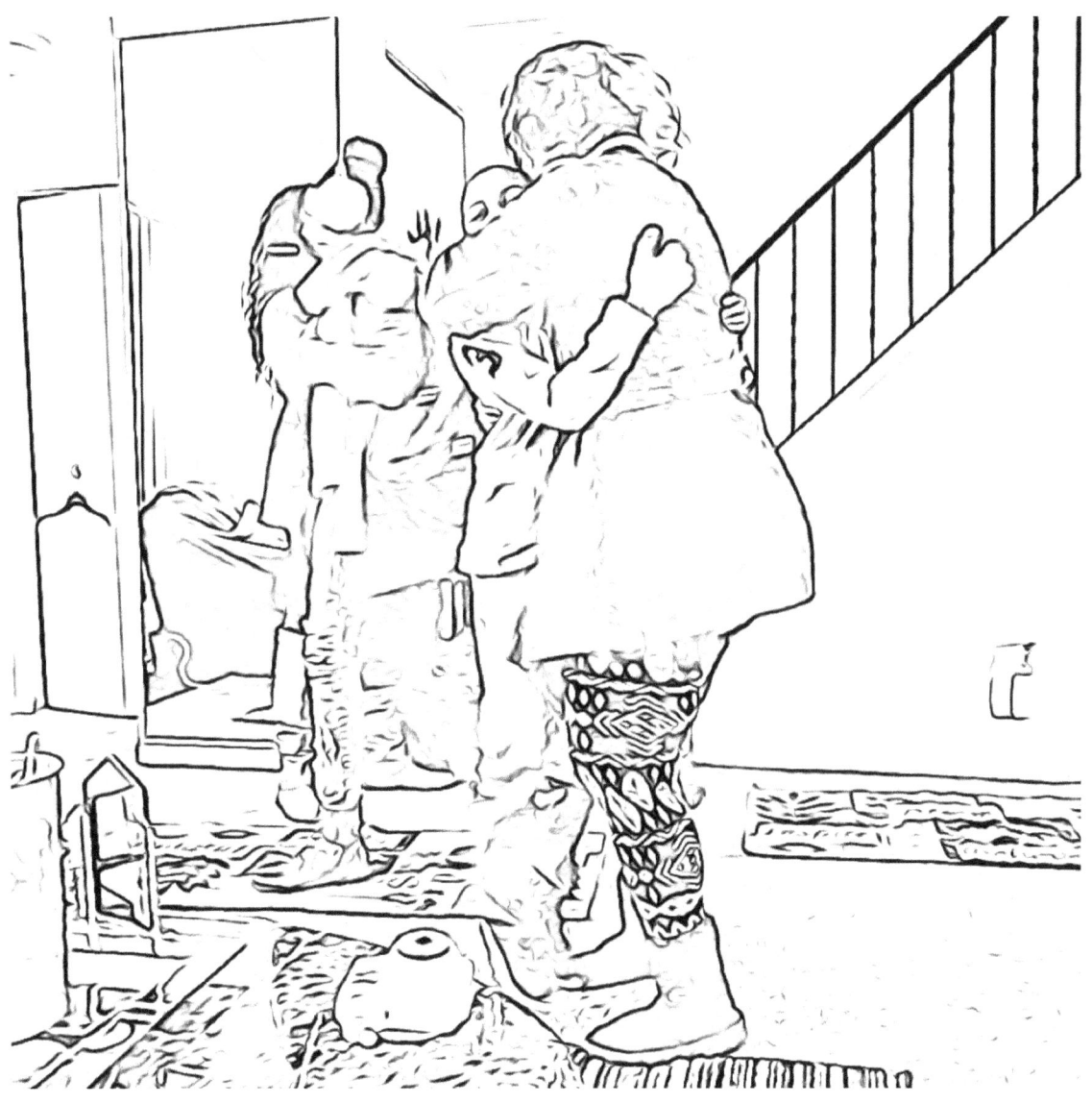

Your life has great worth and value. Always understand someone loves you and if no one has told you, God loves you deeply.

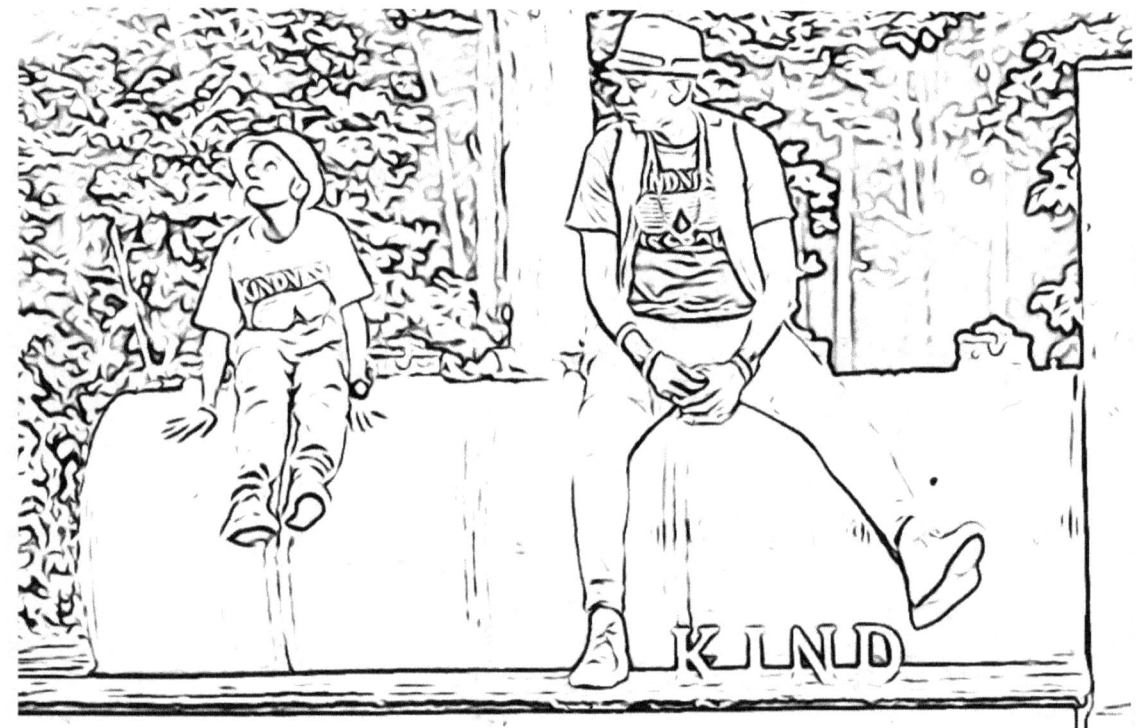

Everyday there are people who wake up just to see your beautiful face. You are loved and Kindness is all around you. Even when you are not aware Kindness is watching out for you and Kindness Is Cool.

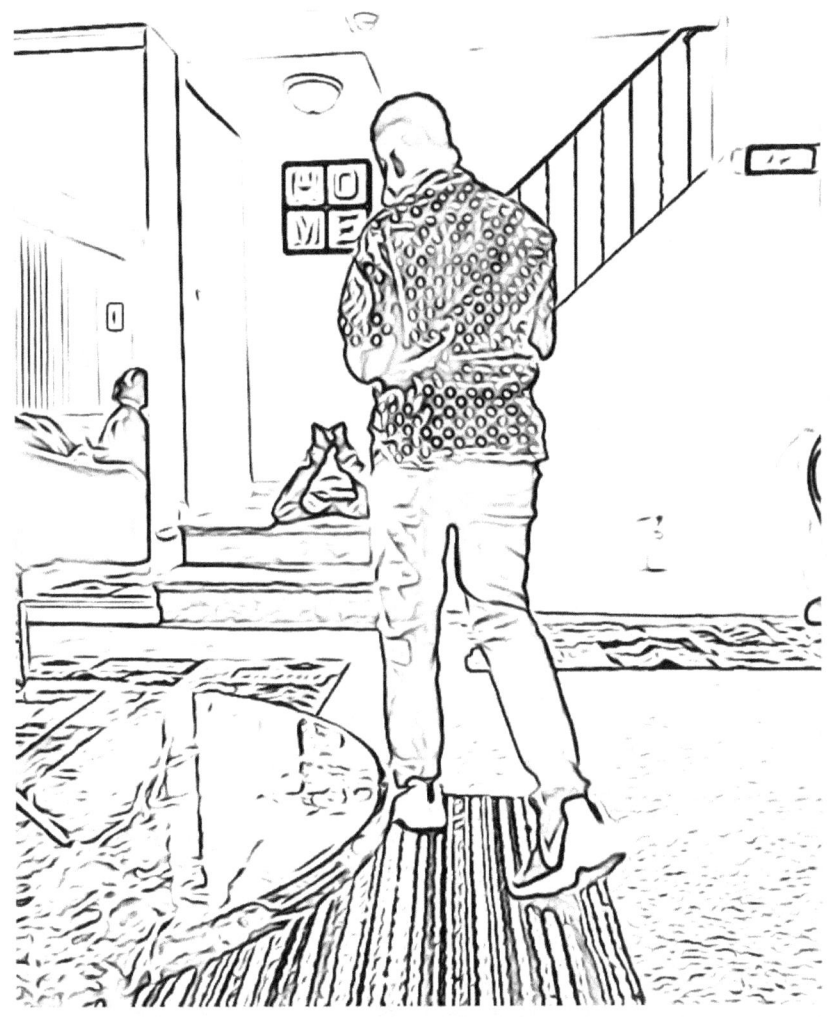

You are not alone and even if you said things that were not nice. You can always go back and try to fix it with new Kind words. Bullying stops when you start being Kind to others.

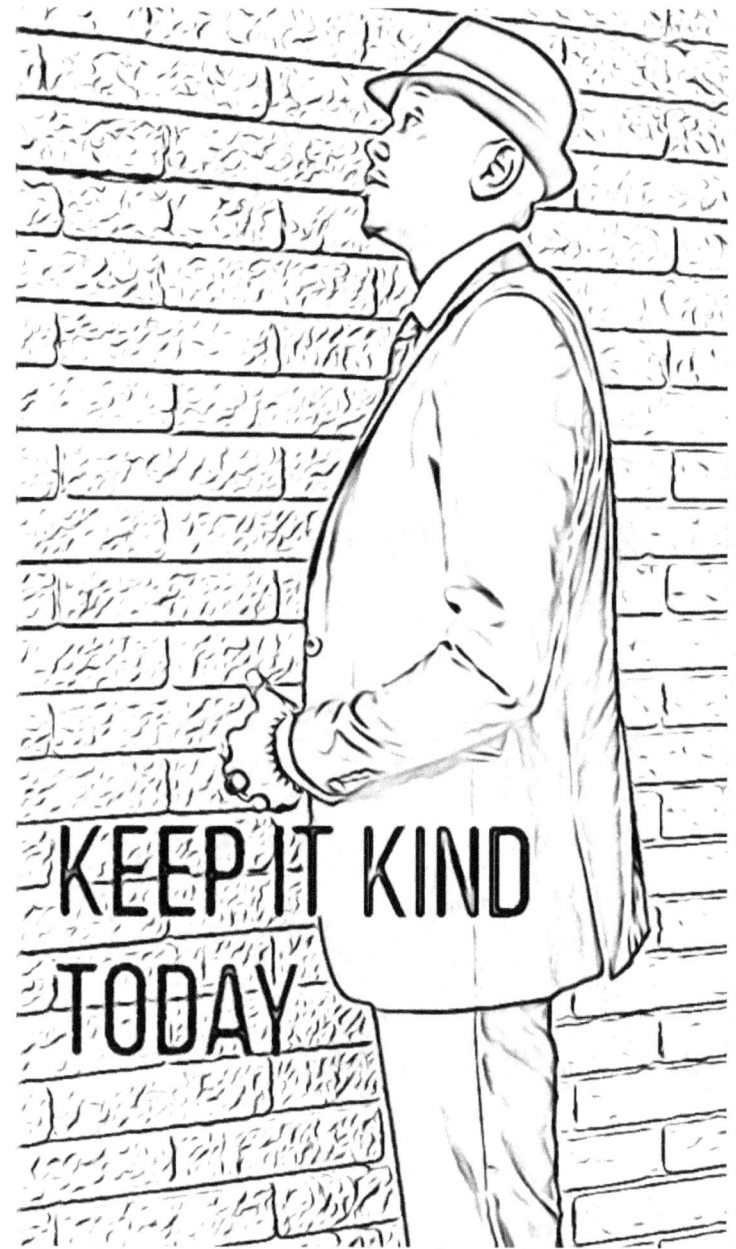

Technology allows us access to strong voices of reason. We need all the help we can get to promote the message of Kindness to others.

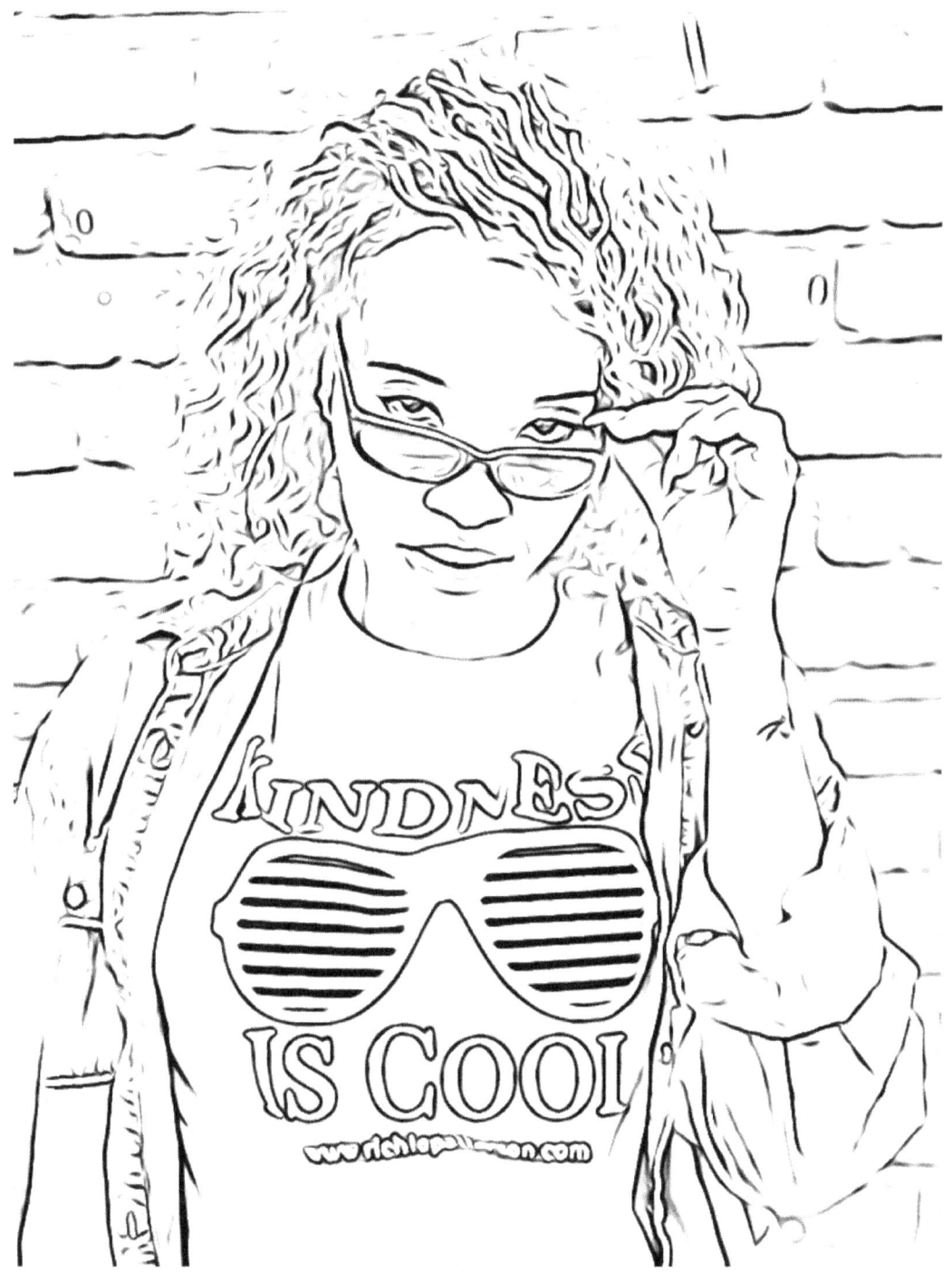

Say it with me, Kindness Is Cool. Kindness Is Cool!!!!!!!!

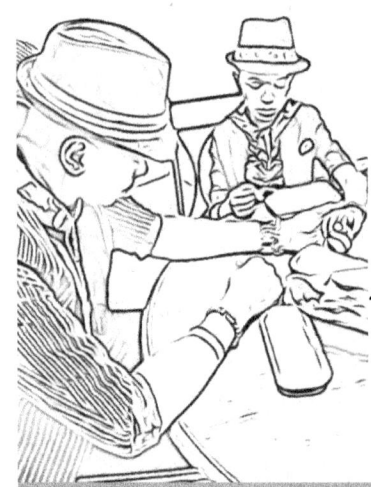

Adressing ADHD through coloring Therapist recommended

Cultivating creativity & family values through coloring
www.richiepatterson.com

#THISISTHEKINDNESS #COLORINGWITHKINDNESS

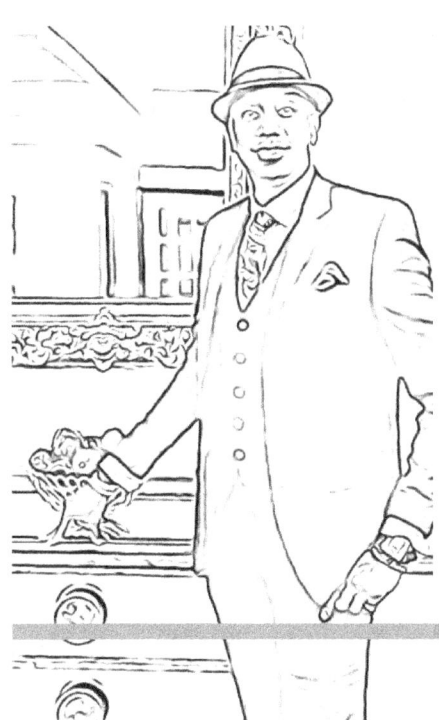

Available for Workshops, Speaking Engagements, Open Forums, Counseling Sessions And More

Pastor Richie Patterson III
8225 Allen Rd #1018
Allen Park, MI 48101
248.372.9500
www.richiepatterson.com

#THISISTHEKINDNESS
#COLORINGWITHKINDNESS

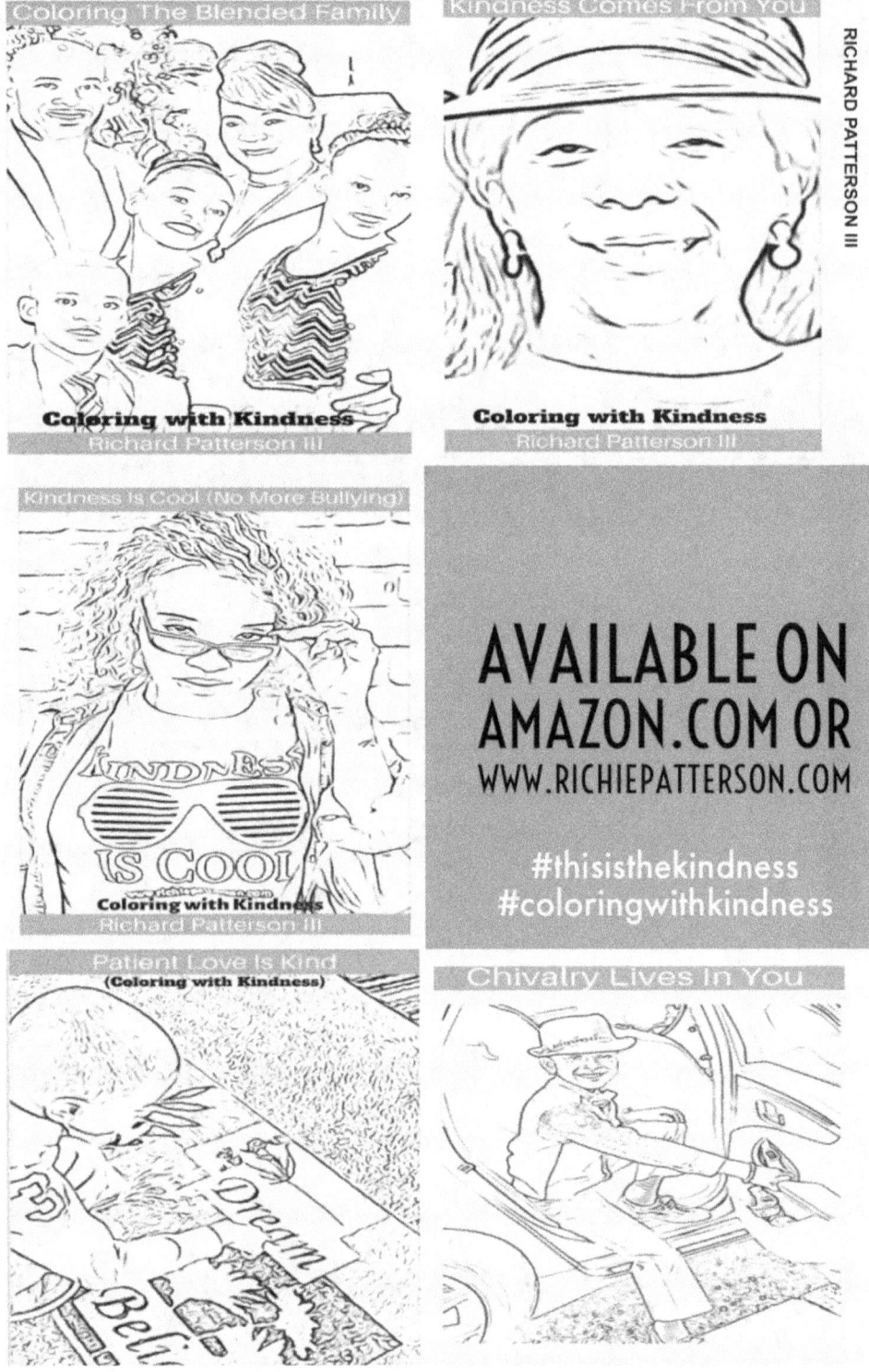

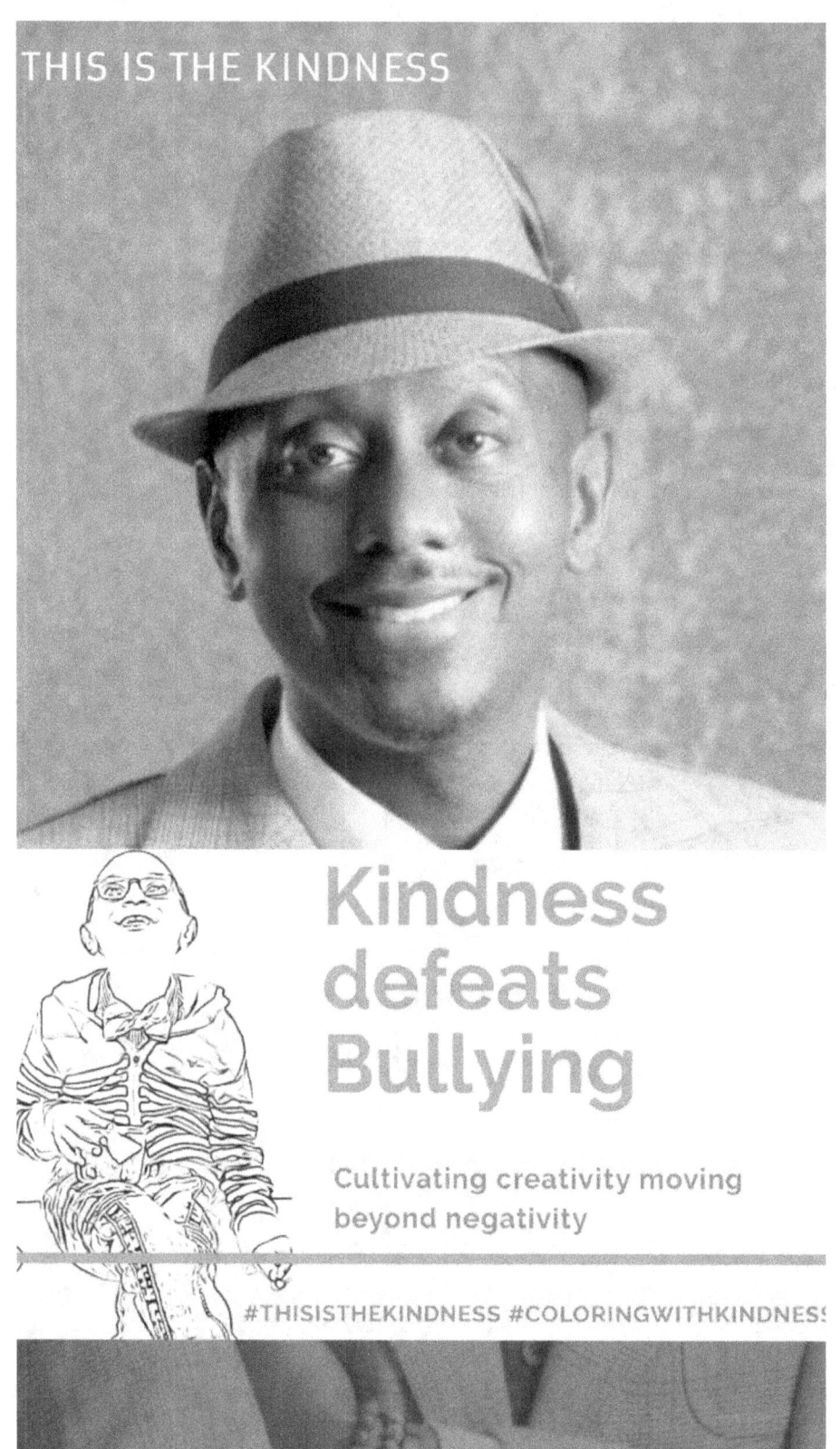

Kindness Is Cool (No More Bullying)

Kindness Is Cool (No More Bullying)

www.ingramcontent.com/pod-product-compliance
Lightning Source LLC
Chambersburg PA
CBHW062337220526
45469CB00008B/2751